# CARICATURES OF THE NPA
# PERSONALITY TYPES

# CARICATURES OF THE NPA PERSONALITY TYPES

## A.M. BENIS, Sc.D., M.D.

**A.M. BENIS**
New York

*One reads that no one exactly resembles anyone else, and that every man is unique, and in a way this is true, but it is a truth easy to exaggerate: in practice men are very much alike. They are divided into comparatively few types.*

— Somerset Maugham (1938)


*We must consider at least three subdivisions of the "expansive type": the narcissistic, the perfectionistic and the arrogant-vindictive type.*

— Karen Horney (1950)

# CONTENTS

# ILLUSTRATIONS

# PREFACE

In this book we present vignettes of character types according to a theory of personality that is based on genetic traits. The vignettes are presented in the form of caricatures, which in fact are excerpts from a chapter entitled *Character Caricatures* of our work first published in 1985 and recently reprinted in an expanded version under the title of *NPA Theory of Personality.*

Scientifically speaking, personality research has not made much progress in the past decades. There are still more theories of personality than there are religions... which means that there is no consensus at all as to which approach is the correct one. Most of the theories are fuzzy and empirical, and not amenable to being either proved or disproved.

Our approach is unique in that it is based on discrete, clearly defined biological traits that are posited to have genetic origins. That is, each of three NPA traits is posited to have an underlying gene. The three traits in various assortments give rise to a limited number of "personality types", and the purpose of this book is to describe each of the types and show how the behavior of each of the types arises quite naturally from the underlying traits.

Do our "NPA types" correspond to reality? Does one of the types appropriately describe... you? We leave it to the reader to decide and to offer an opinion.

The reader may have heard the conventional wisdom that "there are *many genes* underlying personality but *no gene* contributes more than a few percent of any effect". Don't believe a word of it. Everyone knows that a child can inherit the same "personality type" as in one of the parents. There are striking examples of this in my family and very likely in yours as well. If *many genes* were involved, a child's inheriting the "entire packet" of personality genes from just one parent would be an extremely rare event!

Why have scientists not identified the genes corresponding to the NPA traits? The main reason is that geneticists have not yet looked for them. If one doesn't know what one is looking for, one is not likely to find it.

One doesn't have to involve oneself in genetic theory to appreciate that the "caricatures" presented in this book are more just frivolous accounts of haphazard behavior. But for those readers who wish to delve more deeply, we have provided a synopsis of the NPA model in Appendix A, as well as a bibliography that cites our work and also includes the basic references that induced us to formulate the NPA model. These include the works of Karen Horney, to which we make frequent reference. We also include in Appendix B our interpretation of Horney's "morbid dependency" as it applies to NPA types who have the trait of aggression.

Finally, following the example of Horney, we use mainly masculine pronouns to describe the character types, although the descriptions apply equally to males and females. Unfortunately, in the English language there is no good way to avoid this.

AMB
10th September 2018

# INTRODUCTION
## The NPA Model

$\mathbf{T}$he NPA model of personality was developed on the basis of concepts put forth over sixty years ago by German-American psychiatrist Karen Horney [1]. According to the theory, there are three major genetically determined character traits that form the basis of personality. The traits are sanguinity (N), perfectionism (P) and aggression (A). The traits are multifaceted, or in formal terms, each one "dependent on a pleiotropic gene". The notation N is used for the trait of sanguinity, since it has a direct relation to the classic concept of "narcissism".

The traits N and A are posited to be related to branches of the autonomic nervous system, with the trait P being a mediator of the N and A traits. A premise of the model is that in any individual either the trait N or A, or both, must be expressed.

### Three genetically determined traits

Sanguinity (N) is the trait of sociability. Individuals with the trait tend to be prone to flushing, blushing and tearfulness. A hallmark of the trait is the *gingival smile* broadly exposing gums and teeth [2]. In the extreme, the trait appears as a "search for glory", and individuals may display vanity, exhibitionism and show overt narcissistic behavior. Individuals having trait N are called "sanguine" types and sometimes, appropriately, "narcissistic" types.

Aggression (A) is the well-known trait of competitiveness, often physical in nature. Individuals having the A trait (but lacking the N trait) tend to be inhibited in sociability and in flushing, blushing, tearfulness and smiling. In the extreme, the trait is a "search for power", and individuals may display physical confrontation, pugnacity and show overtly sadistic behavior.

Individuals with the trait of aggression instinctively form "pecking orders". Individuals having trait A but lacking trait N are called "non-sanguine" types.

Perfectionism (P) is a trait that may or may not be present in a given individual. It may be thought of as modulating the traits N and A. Individuals having overt expression of the P trait tend to value order, neatness and symmetry, and may be prone to repetitive mannerisms. In the extreme, the trait may be the cause of obsessive-compulsive or autistic-like behavior that may overwhelm other character traits. Individuals lacking trait P are called "non-perfectionistic".

Traits A and N are associated with rage reactions, namely the classic "aggressive-vindictive rage" (A rage) mediated by the sympathetic nervous system and associated with pallor in individuals of light skin color, and the florid "narcissistic rage" (N rage) associated with sanguinity. The P trait is not associated with a rage reaction.

The traits A and N form the basis of human ambition, namely the desire to achieve power and glory, respectively.

An important result is that the model produces a limited number of discrete character types, according to how the three traits are assorted, and whether the traits are present, absent, or incompletely expressed. On the assumption that the three traits assort independently, we identify several main categories of character types: 1) Dominant, 2) Passive Aggressive and 3) Resigned.

## Dominant types

Considering the case where all three traits are either absent or fully expressed, we obtain:

N    sanguine
NP    sanguine perfectionistic
NA    sanguine aggressive
NPA    sanguine perfectionistic aggressive
PA    non-sanguine perfectionistic aggressive
A    non-sanguine aggressive

We note that there are four sanguine types and two non-sanguine types, as well as four aggressive types and two non-aggressive types.

## Passive Aggressive types

If trait A is incompletely expressed, we obtain the category of Passive Aggressive types. The term "passive aggressive" here simply means that expression of trait A is partially inhibited by genetics or environment. We append one minus sign (–) or two minus signs (=) to the letter A, according to whether trait A is only partially or profoundly inhibited.

We obtain the following sanguine Passive Aggressive types:

NA– NA= non-perfectionistic
NPA– NPA= perfectionistic

Passive Aggressive types may be prone to submissive behavior. For purposes of identification, we call the A= types *compliant* types and the A– types *non-compliant* types. In dominant-submissive relationships, non-compliant types can play either the dominant or submissive role, depending on the partner, while compliant types will always seek to play the submissive role.

## Resigned types

If trait A is stunted after maturity because of environmental constraints, we obtain the category of avoidance, or resignation. Unlike the Passive Aggressive types who readily involve themselves in the relative competition of dominance and submission (and sometimes sadomasochism), Resigned types remain detached from such activities and only with difficulty can be stressed to an energetic state of aggression. However, like the Passive Aggressive types, Resigned types do have the capacity to be induced into the aggressive-vindictive "A rage".

Denoting the state of resignation by –A, we obtain the following sanguine Resigned types:

N–A   non-perfectionistic
NP–A   perfectionistic

## Borderline types

Borderline types are those in whom neither trait N nor trait A is fully expressed. These constrained types are relatively uncommon and are not further explored here. For further information on this category and its possible relation to mental illness, see *Synopsis of NPA theory* (Appendix A).

## Sanguine types and aggressive types

Character types are denoted *sanguine* or *non-sanguine* depending on the presence or absence of the trait N, respectively. The two Dominant non-sanguine types are A and PA.

Character types are denoted *aggressive* or *non-aggressive* depending on the presence or absence of the trait A. The two Dominant non-aggressive types are N and NP.

## Mode of genetic transmission of NPA traits

To understand and use the NPA model of personality types, it is not necessary to know the genetic mechanisms underlying the theory. In previous work we have posited that both non-sanguinity and the P trait are transmitted in a Mendelian dominant manner. Thus, a non-sanguine individual must have at least one parent who is also non-sanguine. Similarly, an individual with the P trait must have at least one parent who also has the trait. For further information, see Appendix A.

## Caricatures of the NPA types

This book focuses on detailed description of the most common NPA character types in the form of *caricatures*, as excerpted from our earlier work [1]. Note that the descriptions are meant to greatly magnify the specific characteristics, and foibles, of the various types and are not meant to be taken literally. The pejorative aspects of the descriptions may be considered to be the potential "worst" qualities of the various types. Sometimes a particular behavioral characteristic that seems unfavorable in one social context turns out to be quite advantageous in another. None of the types are presented to be any better or worse than any other. Humans are cognitive beings, and there is much more to personality and behavior than just being male or female, or having a particular assortment of the NPA traits.

## Biological variability and outliers

Just as all males and all females are not alike, there is considerable variability in the characteristics of a given genetic NPA type, say an NP type. This is mainly because of 1) "other genes" that influence behavior, and 2) environment. Environmental influences on behavior can be enormously complex, and could include such diverse factors as the conditions existing during fetal development, "nurture", cultural influences, as well as the individual's real life situation in his or her society.

In the extreme, one should be aware that "outliers" can certainly exist. An outlier is an individual of a certain NPA type who has some unusual attributes that seem "out of character" for that particular type. There are two main reasons for outliers. First, the individual may have unusual genes that rarely occur in the general population or may have been exposed to unusual environmental incidents. Second, the individual may simply have an unusual combination, or "perfect storm", of commonly occurring genes or environmental exposures.

## Some generalizations

Despite our appreciation of "biological variability", we have nevertheless attempted to list trends for such categories as *complexion, gestures, handwriting, sexuality*, and so on. These generalizations should be viewed with caution, since they are, at best, trends in a statistical sense, and could not be used to infer anything about a particular individual. These "trends" have not been confirmed in any scientific sense.

In the context of population genetics, we comment on where geographically the various NPA types are especially prevalent. We introduce the term *habitancy* for a subpopulation of a particular NPA type. For details, see Appendix A.

Finally, we have added a category called "pitfalls". This is a comment on how that particular NPA type might be confused with a different type. There are many reasons why confusion between two types might arise, but the primary reason is that two different types can show overlap in one, or even two, of the NPA traits.

And so, onward to our gallery, starting with the N type…

[*DonkeyHotey*]

# 1

# N type

**"Sanguine type"**

**Sanguine, non-perfectionistic, non-aggressive type**

N types are typically extroverted, sanguine complexioned, non-perfectionistic, and prone to narcissistic posturing and adornment. Low temperament individuals can be soft-spoken, gallant or angelic. High temperament individuals can be charismatic, or intrusive, overbearing and brash. The N type is quite common in politics, aristocratic families and in all lists of famous people, especially in the arts.

**Phenotype**: N

**Genetics:** based on the N trait being recessive

**Animal Model:** bonobo

**Inheritance pattern:** An N type must have at least one parent who is either an N or an NP type. Parents who are both N types can have only N or NA children.

**Infertility:** Increased probability of miscarriages and stillbirths when mated with either an A or PA type.

**Rage:** Narcissistic rage (florid rage resembling a childish tantrum).

**Also known as:** Sanguine, narcissistic personality. The non-aggressive non-perfectionist. The self-anointed glory seeker. Charismatic personality. "Narcissus".

**Complexion:** Sanguine, florid, flushed to blood-red in individuals of light skin color. Blushes easily.

**Smile:** Radiant "gingival" smile, broadly exposing gums and teeth.

**Photograph:** Looks at camera. Broad charismatic gingival smile. Starry-eyed smile.

**Voice:** Confident, smooth, unctuous, pontificating.

**Gestures:** Deep bow, accompanied by sweeping arm. "Narcissistic arms gesture" in which the arms are extended to the front or sides, with the palms up and the fingers somewhat spread apart. It is a pose often assumed by singers and by religious leaders. "Joan of Arc pose" in which the individual's eyes are directed toward the heavens when accepting recognition in the limelight.

**Handwriting:** Very variable. May be beautifully well formed with flourishes, but non-perfectionistic. May be illegible scribbling, especially in male. Exhibitionistic signature ("John Hancock") is common.

**Sexuality:** Tendency to promiscuity: high. Tendency to LGBT in sexual orientation: relatively high.

**Color preference:** Red, especially deep red, is the darling color of the N type.

**Population genetics:** "The Sublime Habitancy", having a high prevalence of N types, some NP types, and very few types having the trait of aggression. Examples: South Sea Islanders, natives of Hawaii and indigenous East Africa.

**Susceptibilities:** Narcissistic personality disorder (NPD), megalomania, messianism. Attention deficit disorders (ADD, ADHD). Unfocused personality. Borderline personality disorder. Confidence man/woman. Vagabond. Uncontrollable florid rages. Munchausen syndrome. Down's syndrome parent. Congenital or rheumatic heart disease. CVA (stroke). Anorexia nervosa, bulimia. Bipolar depression.

**Pitfalls:** Until their lack of compulsive perfectionism becomes apparent, N types can resemble NP types. High temperament, seductive N types can mimic NA types. Loud N types (especially male) can be confused with NPA types. Sexually profligate NP or NPA types could possibly be mistaken for N types. N types with insipient psychosis can exhibit behavior that resembles aggression. Criminal violence in sociopathic N types can lead to mistaken conclusion of A trait.

### *From Chapter 5: A model of human behavior* [3]

He would convey the impression that "I will be the greatest, the most glorious and the most beautiful, and in fact I think that I already am!" He is self-admiring. He has great ambitions with regard to future accomplishments, but does not recognize his limitations. His eyes are set more toward himself and toward the limelight of recognition to be attained in the future than toward the actual tasks with which he must deal. His voice is soothing and clear, and may be directed toward the horizon where all can hear it. His pride is also invested in the beauty of his physical body when in the presence of others. With his not so subtle body postures, mannerisms, and self-congratulatory laughter, he flaunts himself.

Lacking perfectionist qualities, he may have difficulties in organizing himself. He lacks persistence or staying power. Perfectionism by careful repetitive action is alien to him. He has no aggressive-vindictive qualities, does not "play the game" of dominance and submission and does not become involved in the dependency of subjugation. He does not split his personality to a subdued state. He cannot be incited into an aggressive-vindictive rage.

He cannot tolerate any serious criticism of his qualities, or interference in his ambition to attain the limelight. When frustrated he may, on the one hand, be incited into the narcissistic "N rage" of defense and withdrawal, or on the other hand, he may undergo a depression to an abject state of hopelessness.

Aristotle in his *Nicomachean Ethics* gives us a character sketch of the narcissistic personality [4].

Note that we have discovered the personality type of the proselytizing evangelist or the self-anointed prophet. The important qualities of such a personality are as follows. First, he does not recognize his limitations, and his glorious goals become frank delusions of grandeur. Second, lacking perfectionist qualities, he does not occupy himself with the fine details of the means by which his goals are to be attained. For this he requires disciples and other followers to rally around him for the Cause. Third, he is self-anointed; thus, in glorifying his Cause, he is in inverted terms glorifying himself. Finally, lacking aggressive qualities, he is not only sexually unaggressive but also essentially defenseless against attack. If brought before a tribunal he can only repeat in direct or inverted terms that he is the anointed one. And if maltreated and physically abused, he can but turn the other cheek. If led to the gibbet or burned at stake, the anointed one will die the death of a passive martyr, all the while hearing inner voices reassuring him that in the glory of his death lies the glory of his purpose in life.

### *From Chapter 6: Character caricatures* [3]

He is the epitome of unbridled narcissism. Hence, his complexion tends to be sanguine and his smile sublime. If he is at all handsome or beautiful, or even if he is not, he will adorn himself in finery. The female, especially, will not be able to resist wearing colorful clothes or painting her face in a manner that may startle onlookers. If the opportunity arises to flaunt his body in the nude, or semi-nude, he will not be able to resist it. Thus, he displays immense vanity with regard to personal appearance, for example in matters of cleanliness and hair style, but there his punctiliousness stops. In other matters, we shall see, he is flamboyant and extravagant, but as he rides his tiger through life he never seems to achieve any true sense of order or stability.

In placid circumstances this individual is a friendly, unaggressive, perennially optimistic, often charming individual who becomes radiant like a sunflower when flattered. Rather than be embarrassed by adulation, he will revel in it. Whatever his station in life, he will not be able to resist the temptation to mount the podium if the opportunity presents itself. If he has even mediocre talent, he will be a compulsive jokester, a mimic, an amateur singer, or will play some kind of musical instrument. If he has real talent or physical beauty, he will be inexorably drawn to a career in the field of fashion modeling, in the performing arts or in show business. Alternatively he may be drawn to any one of the professions where public oratory is possible. He may thus be a politician, a social activist or an evangelist. As an engineer, a businessman or a physician his genuinely friendly manner may mystify those with whom he comes in contact. They may think his extroverted affectations to be somewhat strange, and may consider him to be either incredibly naive, incredibly conceited or simply groutheaded.

If he inverts his mannerisms of self-importance, he shows no trace of conceit. He presents himself as a dedicated individual with a soothing, self-assured manner. The male may have a starry-eyed appearance and may be accused of being elfish, effeminate or "flaky". The female may be described as "angelic" or "dreamy". If his voice is loud, which it often is in the male, it is a voice of hollowness rather than forcefulness, as if it were a clarion call being delivered into the void around him

Although he is not predatory in a sexual manner, he is extremely vulnerable to flattery and may seek adulation. Hence, he is prone to attracting sycophantic parasites and may even develop intimate physical relations with adulators of the same sex. He may present himself as a sexually promiscuous person but in a naive and ingenuous manner. More than sexual pleasure, he needs the constant reassurance of the opposite sex that he is indeed the wonderful person of his dreams. To others, therefore, he or she appears to have the amorality of innocence, rather than of vice.

As an unaggressive individual, the N type may, at first blush, be confused with the NP type. However, the NP type tends to be poker-faced or melancholic, and tends to work by himself in a perfectionistic manner. The N individual, on the contrary, tends to be buoyant, self-assured, jocular, expansive or even charismatic, and tends to seek people out in order to enlist their aid in his projects. Thus, the NP individual will work quietly to solve a particular problem, while the N individual will organize a conference so that he may lead a discussion on how his ideas may be implemented.

In competitive society, it may be difficult to avoid him, for although he is not aggressive he is obtrusive. He may precede his visit with a letter, definitely written in the first person, describing his extraordinary talents, the fine things that he has done in the past, despite all odds against him, and the grand things that he hopes to accomplish, nay will accomplish. He stands proud, tends to flaunt his body, and projects his resonant voice not only to his partner in conversation, but also to anyone within earshot, or even beyond. His objectives may be grandiose and far beyond the limits of reasonableness in relation to his present status in life.

Any new activity or new person arriving on the scene arouses his great interest, and he will not be able to resist imposing himself on others, ostensibly to see if he can help. And he wishes to help because he believes that he has the qualities and talents to help. On close examination, though, it is he who desires assistance, and his favors done to others reflect this ulterior motive, especially with regard to long-range assistance in his career. And in the background, deep in his unconscious mind, there lives a pervasive suspicion that perhaps all those glorious deeds will never come to fruition. Hence, he requires constant reassurance from others of his worth to them.

What emerges in this character type is an individual who has everything invested in the attainment of the fruits of his ambition, namely in the attainment of the limelight. However, lacking perfectionist qualities, he lacks the ability to apply himself to the finer details of the tasks to be done. This may not be obvious to others at first because he does indeed have boundless energy, and he may seem to have endless "persistence" when it comes to adorning himself or his abode to "perfection", often to the point of garishness. And, it is true, he may be an enthusiastic author when it comes to writing his autobiography or other epic, soaring literary efforts that glorify himself in direct or in barely camouflaged inverted terms. Nevertheless, despite such occasional activities of self-glorification, where he appears to be motivated, dynamic and goal oriented, on closer examination he lacks the persistence to create a meaningful synthesis of the mass of interrelated details that surround him. He is vague. He may be grossly, illogically imprudent. He has infinite pride in being recognized for his nebulous "creativity". But he is like a Don Quixote who leaps onto his horse and tries to gallop off in four directions at once.

For the N type the ends justify the means, and in fact, he would rather not have to bother with the means at all! We see, then, that he judges people not even so much for their potential for future accomplishments as for their already proven abilities to deliver the goods to him. And, of course, his estimation of others varies in direct proportion to the reassurance, deference and outright flattery that they give him.

Having so much invested in attainment of the limelight, once he arrives there it may be difficult to ease him out. His showmanship may take precedence over virtually all other aspects of his character. He may, then, neglect the accepted modalities of human decorum, as he talks endlessly in the first person, and in so doing he inevitably begins to neglect the truth.

Finally, he is vulnerable in the limelight and may be self-destructive there. If he is a sports figure, he may risk his life in attempting a dazzling but dangerous play. And it is he, of course, who will perform the most courageous of courageous acts if they are done in the presence of others, but will be strangely immobile if his noble deed would remain unknown to them.

At work he flaunts himself with his unctuous manner, his ostentatious handwriting and his mellifluous voice. In meetings he arouses resentment in others when he speaks of himself in overt or inverted terms. If others protest, he will not know what they are talking about, for he is the anointed one. And if he is seriously criticized or otherwise frustrated, he will explode into the red-faced narcissistic rage of defense: "I, in fact, am the only one who does anything worthwhile around here!" and of withdrawal: "If you people don't appreciate me, I'm leaving!"

He does not "play the game" of dominance and submission and is not overtly vindictive. If he does raise his voice in frustration to reprimand someone, his bark is but a hollow bellow, and everyone knows it. He is usually a person who would not hurt a fly. His love relations are not based on subjugation but on his conviction of his own beauty, his sexual wiles, and his irresistibility. And in his self-glorification he shows his Achilles heel, for he may become less able to interact meaningfully with those around him, and more and more a prisoner of his own inflated image of himself.

Nevertheless, an individual of the N type may, despite the constraints of his character structure, achieve great success in life. Although lacking the behavioral trait of perfectionism, his narcissistic drive for achievement may allow him to arrive at real accomplishments, especially if his perennial optimism can attract others to help him bring to fruition those dazzling visions of future triumphs.

Those of his acquaintances who do not know him well will be among those who like him the least. They will titter behind his back for his unctuous manner, his conceit, his extravagance and his frivolousness. They may ridicule him for his affected charisma, his perpetual smile, his weakness for empty-headed adulators of either sex, or for his outlandish cosmetics and dress. But those who come to know him more than casually may come to be enchanted by his kindness, his accessibility, his ingenuousness and his impeccable manners.

Individuals of the N type are common in Western society. Illustrious examples may be found in personages such as Lorenzo the Magnificent of the Medici, Marie-Antoinette, Napoleon III and Catherine the Great.

In the works of Somerset Maugham we find examples of females of the N type in the characters of Louise in *The Narrow Corner,* and of Maugham's beloved Rosie in his later novel, *Cakes and Ale.*

As an example of an illustrious N type, the reader is referred to Castelot's perceptive biography of Napoleon's wife, the Empress Josephine [5]. §

[*DonkeyHotey*]

# 2

# A type

**"Aggressive type"**

**Non-sanguine, non-perfectionistic, aggressive type**

A types typically have a non-sanguine complexion, are extroverted, brusque, brash and prone to aggressive arrogance, but not exhibitionistic or narcissistic. The female is sometimes denigrated as "masculine". Circumstances can lead this type to be overtly sadistic. A positive attribute is that he or she gets things done and gets them done fast. Short physical stature is common but not universal.

**Phenotype:** A

**Genetics:** based on A trait being recessive and non-sanguinity (lack of N trait) being Mendelian dominant

**Inheritance pattern:** An A type must have at least one parent who is either an A or a PA type. Parents who are both A types can have only A or NA children.

**Infertility:** Increased probability of miscarriages and stillbirths when mated with either an N or NP character type.

**Rage:** Aggressive-vindictive "A rage" (mass discharge of sympathetic nervous system). Also called the "fight or flight" response.

**Also known as:** Aggressive, choleric personality. "The arrogant dynamo". Non-sanguine autocrat.

**Complexion:** Non-sanguine. Tending toward pallid or sallow in individuals of light skin color. May be milky white. Does not blush easily.

**Smile:** Sardonic smirk. Non-gingival, half-open mouthed grin. Grin with short, repetitive laugh to mask the incapacity to smile.

**Photograph:** Looks at camera. "Pleased-with-self" grin.

**Voice:** Confident, confrontational, abrasive, bullying.

**Gestures:** Clenched fist, aggressive finger point, haughtily-cocked jaw, intimidating glare.

**Handwriting:** Non-perfectionistic. Often slurred or bold illegible scrawl.

**Sexuality:** Tendency to promiscuity: moderate. Tendency to LGBT in sexual orientation: low-moderate.

**Color preference:** Inattentive approach to color choice.

**Population genetics:** "The Militant Habitancy", having a high prevalence of A and PA types. Examples: Yemen, Arab part of Iraq, other Middle Eastern subpopulations.

**Susceptibilities:** Attention deficit disorders (ADD, ADHD). Overt sadism, sociopathology. Antisocial personality disorder. Sadomasochistic "morbid dependency" as the dominant partner. Leader of militant, genocidal movement. "Absolute power corrupts absolutely."

**Pitfalls:** High-temperament PA types can resemble A types. Accounts of the behavior of NPA types or bipolar NA types can resemble A types. Accounts of (pseudo) perfectionist behavior in A type could lead to mistaken conclusion of P trait. A types, in drive for power, may mount the podium, leading to mistaken conclusion of the N trait. "Punky" adornment may lead to mistaken conclusion of the N trait (pseudo-narcissism). Psychosis in N or NP types can superficially resemble aggression and even sadism.

*From Chapter 5: A model of human behavior*

He conveys the impression that "I am the strongest. I come first. Period!" He cannot help but be an extrovert and be overtly arrogant. To him arrogance is power, since in arrogating to himself qualities of special importance, nay of omnipotence, he can self-righteously use the brute force of a steamroller to attain his goals. His hallmark is that of seeking the vindictive triumph in overt intimidation, or indeed in any manner that is available to him. He should be able to do anything to anyone, but no one — but no one — can have any claim on him. He is loud. He cannot be missed. He is first.

He "plays the game" but compulsively must dominate all others. He will avoid at all costs his own subjugation in a personal relationship or in a "morbid dependency"; rather he will be the subjugator. He may split his personality for short periods of time to a subdued state, but will be most unhappy there and will emerge fighting. Having so much invested in aggressive dominance, he will scorn anyone and anything reminiscent of weakness or of submissive tenderness. When opposed, he is the master of vindictive retaliation, and will thirst for the thrill of the vindictive triumph, with strict accountability until retribution is obtained. When attaining subjugation over others he may become sadistic, but his sadism is in the realm of brute force: it is out in the open for all to see. When cornered, with his back to the wall, he will fight and may be at his best.

He has little in the way of narcissistic qualities, hence he has less invested in the anticipation of future accomplishment than in the maintenance of a position of power, where no one can have any claim on him. He has little in the way of perfectionist qualities; therefore, his actions are coarse, with a premium on speedy, goal-oriented, self-obtained satisfaction. He is thus openly hedonistic. Perfectionism by quiet, careful repetitive action is alien to him.

When frustrated, he has in his armamentarium the aggressive-vindictive "A rage", which may be activated with a hair trigger. With repeated defeats he may undergo a depression to an abject state of hopelessness.

### *From Chapter 6: Character caricatures*

His complexion tends to be sallow rather than sanguine. Lacking the sanguine trait, he tends not to adorn himself. But he cannot be missed. He has a loud voice and a brusque demeanor. He is rough around the edges. He is arrogant, aggressive and often cannot help being callous. He is a steamroller who cannot be stopped, or if he is halted, it is only for a moment. He must be first, and no one can have any true claim on him. If he does submit to others, it is he who is magnanimously doing them a favor.

He cuts corners in almost every aspect of his life, in his relations with others, in time, in space, in his poor handwriting and in the realm of the truth. Perfectionist traits of careful, directed activity and of a sense of duty to others are alien to him. He will be happy to say that doing something over and over again to make it better and better will only make it worse and worse. To him it is obvious: perfectionism is the enemy of progress.

He is not by nature a contemplative person; hence, he has only the slightest understanding of the forces that propel him. And it is only for the most fleeting moments of introspection that he wonders why he must so often act like the callous boor that he so often is.

He may not realize it, but his *modus operandi* is a claim of omnipotence. If in his present situation he is not the lord and master, then he tells himself that he soon will be. He "plays the game" of dominance and submission, and to the extent that he considers himself the master of all, his eye contact with others is often poor. Why should he, the all-powerful master, waste his time with eye contact on mere weaklings?

If he is seriously criticized, he will bristle and shoot from the hip. His argumentative reply will not finish until he has achieved a vindictive triumph. He must have the last word.

Just as he does not know how to give thanks or give compliments, he does not know how to apologize. Whatever the issue at hand, truth becomes secondary to an instinctive urge telling him that power must prevail. In fact, in a competitive society he is a dynamo whose meaning, and satisfaction, in life is the vindictive triumph over all individuals, whom in the final analysis he considers to be weaker than he. But satisfaction in life through the vindictive triumph over weaker individuals is, the reader will recall, our definition of sadism, so in the wrong time and the wrong place he is capable not only of the most callous disregard of the rights of others, but also the worst of cruel, sadistic acts [6].

In better circumstances, his aggressive tendencies are out in the open for all to see. His friends, family and acquaintances will come to recognize and predict his vindictiveness and his accountability for retribution like an elephant that never forgets. They will come to be accustomed to his vindictive rages, much like modern city dwellers become accustomed to the sonic boom. And despite his self-devotion, his hedonism, his arrogance, his brashness and his brusqueness, they may like him. This may be because they have sensed that in admiring him, and in letting him know that they admire him, they give him his only link to tenderness in interpersonal relations: personal recognition for his accomplishments. And they learn that this is the only way to gain his fleeting "smile".

Finally, he may be admired by both the strong and the weak for his qualities of getting things done, and getting them done fast. "Damn the torpedoes! Full steam ahead, come hell or high water!"

As a "player of the game" he must be the dominant figure, and so it must be in love relations, which are, of course, usually based on the subjugation of other weaker aggressive or passive aggressive types. And if his daily life is one modest vindictive triumph after another, then his true vindictive rages may be few and far between. He may then be less of an Attila the Hun or a Genghis Khan than a brusque, abrasive dynamo who, despite his being a prisoner of the primeval forces that drive him, charges through life as a useful functioning member of society.

[Carsten S.]

# 3

# NA type

**"Sanguine-aggressive type"**

**Sanguine, non-perfectionistic, aggressive type**

NA types tend to be sanguine-complexioned, hyperactive extroverts. Both traits of ambition, i.e., unbridled narcissism and aggression, are fully manifest. High temperament individuals may be characterized by intemperate behavior not conducive to stable relationships. If the trait of aggression predominates, then the NA type may exhibit sadistic behavior. The NA type often seeks celebrity status, especially in the performing arts.

**Phenotype:** NA

**Genetics:** based on traits N and A both being recessive

**Animal Model:** chimpanzee

**Inheritance pattern:** An NA type can have parents of any combination of the other character types. Two NA types can have children of only NA types (this is the only NPA type that always "breeds true").

**Infertility:** No increased probability of miscarriages and stillbirths when mated with any other character type.

**Rage:** Narcissistic "N rage" (florid rage of sanguinity), or aggressive-vindictive "A rage" (mass discharge of sympathetic nervous system), or combined "NA rage".

**Also known as:** Cyclothymic, histrionic, hysterical or hypomanic-depressive personality. "The ambitious predator". The *prima donna*.

**Complexion:** Tending toward sanguine or flushed in individuals of light skin color. NA types have the capacity to blush but typically are unembarrassable.

**Smile:** Showy, glamorous, toothy smile of movie star.

**Photograph:** Looks at camera. Extroverted, flashy smile.

**Voice:** Confident. Highly-modulated with mini-bursts of rapid-fire speech.

**Gestures:** Active or hyperactive gestures. Often seductive body contact in casual social situations.

**Handwriting:** Variable, non-perfectionistic. Sometimes rounded, elegant letters in female.

**Sexuality:** Tendency to promiscuity: high. Tendency to LGBT in sexual orientation: low.

**Color preference:** Bright yellow, pink, orange, multicolors. Even chartreuse. No particular attraction to red.

**Population genetics:** "The Corybantic Habitancy", having a high prevalence of NA types. Examples: Brazil, Senegal, indigenous Australia, New Guinea.

**Susceptibilities:** Attention deficit disorders (ADD, ADHD). Hysteria, hypochondria, fugues. Hypomanic personality. Histrionic personality disorder. Bipolar disorder. Manic episodes. Explosive rages. Eating disorders. Sadomasochistic "morbid dependency" as the dominant or dependent partner. Narcissistic personality disorder (NPD).

**Pitfalls:** High temperament N types or hyperactive NPA types can resemble NA types. High temperament, zany, pseudo-narcissistic PA types can mimic NA types. A sullen, depressed NA type can resemble a PA type.

### *From Chapter 5: A model of human behavior*

He would synergistically combine the mottos, "I am the most glorious" and "I am the most powerful". Thus, lacking the trait of perfectionism, his life is ruled by the unbridled ambition of the traits of narcissism and aggression. We surmise that these two traits, as expressed separately in the N and A personages, would be found together in this individual.

The synergistic drives for both power and glory must produce an extroverted, hyperactive individual. Given the pride invested in "I am beautiful" and "I am powerful", one would expect this individual to be domineering, with an almost megalomanic drive for ambition, in power, glory and sexual domination. This individual lacks concerted perfectionist qualities, hence his search for power and glory is likely to be superficial, spasmodic and lacking in direction.

When reduced to the subdued state NA− this individual strongly resembles the self-flaunting unaggressive sanguine personage N. Of course, he "plays the game" of dominance and submission, and with his hyperactivity and tendency toward hypersexuality he would involve himself in many compulsive dependencies, usually as the subjugator but sometimes as the subjugated individual. As is often the case in such relationships, he may become overtly sadistic, especially in frustrating and in playing on the emotions of his subjugated companions, of which there may be several at one time. And he too, if opposed, seeks retribution in the self-justified vindictive triumph.

This individual when frustrated can be incited to the "N rage" (truly a narcissistic rage), to the "A rage" (truly an aggressive rage), or to a combined narcissistic-aggressive "NA rage". In the latter, the aggressive-vindictive component usually appears first, followed by the narcissistic rage of withdrawal as the individual leaves, slamming the door behind him.

Finally, as in all character types, he is liable, when frustrated to a point of relative hopelessness, to enter an abject state of depression. In such a hyperactive individual, with ambition unchecked by the lack of perfectionism, we are drawn to propose that he is in some cases the histrionic, cyclothymic, or hypomanic-depressive personality of the psychiatric literature.

### *From Chapter 6: Character caricatures*

This individual is driven by the unbridled instincts of narcissism and aggression, without mediation of these traits by that of perfectionism. Thus, the behavioral qualities found in the N and A types presented previously may also appear in essentially unaltered form in the NA individual. Those qualities will not be repeated in detail here.

This individual is an extrovert, there is no question about that. He usually has a moderately loud voice, but more than loud he is talkative, or outright loquacious. His loquacity is characterized by bursts of rapid speech and has a gossipy quality to it, often with the use of slang expressions, sexual innuendo, and many references to current fads. He is vivacious, flamboyant, flashy, theatrical and somewhat agitated. He may have a hyperactive, labile, mercurial quality and may employ openly seductive body language, accompanied by agitated gestures. He may be in a state of perpetual motion, literally being unable to sit still. Others may comment that "He runs around like a chicken with his head cut off". We might say that he has flounce and he has bounce.

He may be described as charming, but his charm seems to lack any real depth, as if it were a highly-polished artificial veneer. He seems in posture and in manner to be self-assured, but his self-assurance, like his other qualities, seems to be superficial, as if it could be popped like a balloon. In the same way, he may be described as attractive, but more in the literal sense of being capable of attracting the opposite sex, rather than having the attributes of profound beauty. He does not hesitate to talk about any subject, in public or in private, with little regard as to whether it might cause embarrassment to his companion in conversation. In fact, he is practically unembarrassable. He may be "nosey". To use American parlance, "he has a lot of verve and a lot of nerve".

With his agitation and vibrancy, his eye contact with others is often not good, and this is, once more, true to the extent that he feels himself to be above others. His laugh may be loud, penetrating and in the female shrill, but may seem to be forced. He smiles easily. The female can, with especial ease, flash a charming smile at will and hold it indefinitely, as if for a photograph.

As was true for the A type, he is basically aggressive and must dominate over all others, in little matters and in big, in every way and throughout every day. If challenged, or even if not challenged, he may be arrogant, brash and belligerent. If a stressed relationship is to be terminated, whether with a friend, a colleague, an acquaintance or a mate, it must be terminated in the context of a vindictive triumph. And the snarling, vicious, directed vindictive rage is certainly in his repertoire but may rarely be seen.

In his perpetual motion he fills up his time with trips, visits, classes and activities but is not really a "workaholic" in the sense of devoting himself to any real work. He is a dilettante. He is at his best in task-oriented activities. He tends to lack any deep sense of duty. Lacking in perfectionist qualities, he has little staying power. His most reliable attributes are his impulsiveness and his inconstancy.

He is, if you listen to him, intensely ambitious and he may say so in those words, but there is a great discrepancy between his ambitions and his real accomplishments. Sometimes he seems propelled by the jet stream of his own self-generated hot air. He is extravagant. There is a definite proclivity to travel, preferably by airplane, and it seems as if someone else is always paying for his trip. He is an intensely social person, a partygoer, and indeed the classic "life of the party". And as he becomes older, lacking the staying power for satisfying his deep needs for accomplishment and affection, he senses that something is wrong, that perhaps he is not "normal". But more often than not he will acknowledge that of course he is not normal — he is exceptional!

His relations with the opposite sex may be characterized as troublesome, turbulent and tormenting. Although the range of variability in human behavior in the realm of sexuality is enormously wide, there is no question that many of these individuals place a premium on sexuality in their lives. Some of them could well be placed into the bygone categories of satyriasis and nymphomania. He is a coquette, a tease, a bird of prey, a vampire. There may be a continual, compulsive search for sexual partners, ostensibly to satisfy a conscious desire for a stable relationship. Instead, there occurs only one turbulent, tormenting relationship after another, and he views the past in perplexed amazement as he recounts how many partners fell in love with him, how many wanted to marry him, and how many he crushed by leaving them abruptly. Why, oh why, he wonders, cannot he really fall in love? Why, oh why, does he end by treating his partners so scornfully, so sadistically?

The answers to these questions are not difficult to find and lie, of course, in the narcissistic-aggressive character structure itself. His narcissistic self tells him that he is a grand person, thereby laying a framework of conceit. His aggressive, hedonistic instinct tells him that he must dominate his partner and get his pleasure while he can. And in dominating his partner, he cannot give of himself to him. He, thus, cannot provide his partner with the one thing that his partner craves for the most — his tenderness. And as his partner clings to him more and more, all the more there is established a master-slave relationship. The master becomes alienated. His eyes become averted from the slave. And he begins to treat the slave with all of the tormenting, sadistic means that are available to him in the repertoire of muted, and not so muted, aggressive human behavior [7].

The "slave" for his part is usually a weaker Dominant type having an aggressive component or a Passive Aggressive type who becomes literally enslaved in a chronic state of subjugation. Here, it is truly fitting to call the relationship a "morbid dependency", the slave usually being totally incapable of extricating himself, however illogical the situation. The affair ends when the NA master moves on, sometimes sadistically playing off a former partner against his new interest, setting the stage for a new turbulent relationship. And this may be repeated again and again.

If he marries and assumes the dominant role, then the marriage may not portend well. Unless the real life circumstances provide an enormous amount of compensatory cement to the marriage, the master will torment the slave subtly or overtly and finally leave him. If he assumes the subjugated role, then for much of the time lie will resemble the narcissistic N type, and his aggressive component will be strongly muted.

The female of this character type, in modern Western society, may lead a particularly turbulent life. And given her total confusion with regard to the instinctual demons that are propelling her through life like a speedboat out of control, one cannot help but be sympathetic toward her. She feels that she is destined to do great things, but somehow feels that she is not "normal". She wants to work with others, but bitterly resents being asked to do anything for anyone.

She has pride in her beauty, but somehow feels that she is physically flawed. It is perplexing to others how this individual, often frankly attractive, has almost invariably a negative body image of herself, a flaw, whether it be an imperfect complexion, an imperfect nose, this feature or that. Somehow her narcissistic voice demands physical "perfection" of herself. And in response to the disparate feelings of ugliness on the one hand, and the need to be a ravishing beauty on the other, she places an enormous investment in efforts to enhance her physical appearance. There is an emphasis on fashionable, perfectly-matching clothes, with price being no object, on accessories of dress, on her hair style, on nail polish, cosmetics and perfumes, and the like. In some cases this emphasis superficial qualities of personal adornment is so striking that one has the impression that she is gaudily attempting to gild a lily.

With regard to her sexuality, in which there is so much pride invested, total confusion reigns. Being an aggressive type she instinctively scorns weakness, but all the while dreaming of a superman who will overpower her and possess her, she paradoxically seeks men whom she can dominate and subjugate. And in doing so, she almost invariably chooses among those who long for submission. And in dominating she wonders why she cannot submit to true love, why she cannot be tender, and why she is, despite all of her investment in sexuality, often sexually unresponsive. And it is in her unresponsiveness and in her need to dominate all aspects of a sexual relationship — sometimes to the fringes of normality — that one senses her desperation. It the desperation of a person who, despite the whirlwind of activity surrounding her, is essentially alone and forlorn in her life. It is the desperation of a voice crying in the wilderness.

There is little doubt that an individual of the NA type (or N type) has a predilection for an older mate, as has been noted by literary figures of the past. For example, the playwright Henryk Ibsen, at the age of sixty-one, became involved in an affair with a young predatory female, who was to become the character Hilda in two of his plays. We can see, in fact, in Ibsen's play *The Master Builder* [8] the broad outlines of what must have been basic dynamics of Ibsen's relationship with Emilie. The character Solness is clearly Ibsen himself, and although he is the object of Hilda's sexually predatory nature, this aspect is secondary. Solness is, to be sure, a sexual being, and even a father figure, but he is above all Hilda's ideal image of her unbridled ambition. We realize, now, why the NA female is drawn to an older man. It is the ulterior motive of the trait of narcissism that is telling her subliminally: "He is your ideal image. He is your promise of glory. You and he are one and the same. Lose yourself completely in him. Merge with him". Unfortunately, her aggressive nature is telling her, "Dominate him every day and in every way", hence her sadistic impulses may ultimately doom any hopes for a stable relationship.

In competitive society, if a female of this character type attempts to achieve success in a career, and at the same time dominate her erotic sphere, conflicts are bound to arise, as in an example of a letter to a newspaper columnist [9].

But such conflicts are, of course, not ones limited intrinsically to the female. As with other character types, we must ask ourselves whether any individual is, by his basic nature, suitable for a given life situation.

Finally, we reiterate the wide range of emotional behavior of the NA type: his hypomanic highs and his abject depressive lows. He may be prone to obesity as he alternately overeats in splurges and then abstains from food entirely. He is particularly prone to psychosomatic illness, for example to headaches, intestinal problems, palpitations, or attacks of "nervousness". When intimidated he may split his personality abruptly to the NA–subdued state, where he becomes a narcissistic type with not a trace of aggression to be seen! This dramatic personality split, when it occurs, is truly remarkable.

As an example of this emotional lability of the NA type, we refer the reader to Somerset Maugham's short story *Rain,* where we find a young lady of the NA type, Sadie Thompson, abruptly change between a hypomanic state and one of abject depression [*10*].

Finally, if we add to the NA individual's behavioral repertoire the occurrence of the combined narcissistic-aggressive NA rage, we see the extent to which this individual is a captive of his emotions.

[*DonkeyHotey*]

# 4

# NP type

**"Sanguine-perfectionistic type"**

**Sanguine, perfectionistic, non-aggressive type**

NP types are usually reserved, unaggressive individuals, tending toward a sanguine complexion and a propensity to blush easily. The N trait of sanguinity is "bridled" by the P trait, so overt narcissism is absent. This is the dutiful, aloof "quiet achiever" who is obsessive and compulsive with regard to order, symmetry and neatness, often reflected in handwriting. Despite being unaggressive, these individuals can be very stubborn. Low temperament individuals may be described as "rigid", "wooden", "melancholic" or "bovine", while high temperament individuals can be "nervous birds" and may be more prone to intemperate behavior. NP monarchs are sometimes "lambs among the wolves". Tall and lean physical stature is common but not universal.

**Phenotype:** NP

**Genetics:** based on P being a Mendelian dominant trait

**Animal Model:** orangutan, gorilla

**Inheritance pattern:** An NP type must have at least one parent who is either an N or an NP type.

**Infertility:** Increased probability of miscarriages and stillbirths when mated with either an A or a PA type.

**Rage:** Narcissistic "N rage" (florid rage resembling a childish tantrum).

**Also known as:** Narcissistic-perfectionist personality. Obsessive-compulsive personality. Phlegmatic-melancholic or bovine personality. "Nervous bird" personality. "The quiet achiever".

**Complexion:** Tending toward sanguine or flushed in individuals of light skin color. Prone to blush very easily.

**Smile:** Uncommon sudden warm, radiant sheepish smile. Sometimes gingival smile (broadly exposing gums and teeth). The gingival smile is striking when seen, but may be rare, especially in melancholic individuals.

**Photograph:** Looks at camera. Relaxed face; sheepish, sometimes radiant "limelight" smile.

**Voice:** Confident, measured, deferential.

**Gestures:** Sometimes "narcissistic arms" gesture in which the arms are extended in front of the individual, with palms up and the fingers somewhat spread apart. It is a pose often assumed by singers and by religious leaders when praising their gods.

**Handwriting:** Almost invariably well-formed, with each letter clearly legible. Sometimes striking calligraphic quality. Sometimes tiny, well-formed letters.

**Sexuality:** Tendency to promiscuity: very low. Tendency to LGBT in sexual orientation: very low.

**Color preference:** Subdued colors. Dark blue, black, white, black-and-white, beige. Tends to avoid bright red, especially in female.

**Population genetics:** "The Punctilious Habitancy", having a high prevalence of NP types and very few A or PA types. Examples: Switzerland, Germany, Scandinavia, Taiwan.

**Susceptibilities:** Obsessive-compulsive personality disorder (OCPD). Narcissistic personality disorder (NPD, may be masked by individual's perfectionist trait). Tantrums. "Control freak".

Hoarding disorder. Unipolar, postpartum depression. Compulsive criminal. Autism or Asperger syndrome. Epilepsy. Leukemia. Rheumatic and congenital heart disease. Down's syndrome parent. Varicose veins, hemorrhoids, stroke. Coronary artery disease is rare.

**Pitfalls:** Can be mistaken for PA type, or Passive Aggressive NPA− or NPA= type. High temperament individuals can superficially resemble NPA+ types. An NP type in a position of authority can be a rigid disciplinarian, meting out severe punishment (pseudo-aggression). The compulsive need for "control" may be misinterpreted as the "thirst for power". In imminent psychosis the hyperactive behavior of the NP type can mimic aggressive behavior. Not all NP individuals of light skin color have a baseline sanguine (pinkish) complexion: it may lack color.

### *From Chapter 5: A model of human behavior*

This individual has narcissistic qualities that are mediated by the trait of perfectionism. Thus, he has narcissistic ambition ("I will be glorious") but also perfectionistic qualities ("Do it well..."). This individual would be well motivated, but a perfectionist plodder. He would be slow. He would do it over and over again. He would chip away at something ever so slowly, so he will not go too fast, or too far all at once. He must be something of a loner. He must be somewhat subdued. He fills up his time with activities, doing, redoing, starting, not quite finishing, polishing, giving him a "workaholic" quality. His time may be filled with ambitious goals, but slow repetitive actions, so that he is always late for appointments. We propose that he may be one of the so-called obsessive-compulsive individuals of the psychiatric literature.

He has his eye on the limelight, to be sure, with a vision toward the future. But the self-flaunting aspect of the previously described narcissistic N type is mediated by this individual's necessity to be perfect in all ways. Thus, the conceit of the narcissistic individual is moderated into persistent achievement in quiet modesty. In fact, this individual feels that he must do whatever his friends, family and society demand of him as a perfect person. He simply must try to do to the best of his ability what he feels he should do. And he feels that he should do everything. And do it perfectly. Thus, to his friends, to his family and to himself, he is a prisoner of his own sense of duty. He is a quiet achiever but at the same time a prisoner of perfection.

Although the traits of narcissism and perfectionism appear to be acting in concert, it is apparent that the demands of modern society can lead to great conflicts in this character type. Narcissism gives him the vision of a glorious future and the possibility of the limelight, while perfectionism is the root of his excruciating, painstakingly slow progress. In addition, no human being can possibly accomplish in the time of twenty-four hours all that he expects of himself, not to mention all the demands that others place on him.

Lacking aggressive qualities, he is defenseless against aggressive types. He does not "play the game" of dominance and submission, does not split his personality to a subdued state, and cannot be induced into an aggressive-vindictive rage. He is not sexually aggressive in a predatory manner. Since his love relations cannot be based on a dominant-submissive relationship, he loves on the basis of his narcissistic and perfectionist qualities. In particular, he loves because he should love, and he is tender because he should be tender. In fact, he will do anything that a devoted mate should do, simply because his inner nature tells him, "I deserve it to myself and to everyone that I should do everything perfectly."

In essence, his attitude in its compulsive rigidity becomes equivalent to a "deal with life". If he pays attention to all the details of life, if everything is neatly in its place, if he has thought of everything in advance, then nothing should go wrong. And when things do go wrong, whether they are by any stretch of the imagination his fault or not, he blames himself for not having foreseen the difficulty. This may send him to the doldrums of a melancholic abject state for days or months, especially if the cause of the failure actually was some deficiency on his part.

He may be incited to the perfectionistic-narcissistic rage when frustrated by others. This begins as a few moments of inwardly directed seething, and then may break out into an agitated narcissistic "N rage" of defense and withdrawal.

Finally, we note that in the NP character structure we expect to find a quiet, unaggressive individual who should be content with perfecting the various aspects of his life with a minimum of conflict with others. However, in a poorly adjusted individual his inner voices may demand of him an incessant repetition of bizarre acts, so that he may attempt to satisfy some poorly-understood need for order or completeness in his life. If these acts come into conflict with the norms of his society, then he may become a compulsive gambler or bank robber, a kleptomanic collector, or even a ritualistic murderer. Hence, such an individual, although lacking the aggressive behavioral trait, could certainly be branded as "aggressive" by his society.

### From Chapter 6: Character caricatures

We will describe the NP type with the understanding that the baseline temperament of these individuals may vary widely, from the "phlegmatic" to the "nervous".

If one were required to describe this individual as an introvert or extrovert, one would tend to say that he is a quiet, friendly, sincere, somewhat sheepish introvert. He is polite, dependable, calm, careful, conscientious, considerate and cooperative. He is modest, pleasant and cheerfully reserved. He may have a pensive, bashful quality. He is unselfish, tolerant and sympathetic. He is neat and scrupulously attentive to detail. His desk is usually neat, his affairs are in order, and his dress, although not necessarily fashionable, is impeccable. He does not have an unbridled need to adorn himself. He may have a fetish for order, symmetry, neatness, with a place for everything and everything in its place. His handwriting is usually highly legible, with every letter clearly visible. It may have a calligraphic quality. A piece of work imperfectly done or lying unfinished causes him no end of smoldering grief. He may be a compulsive house cleaner.

He has a strong sense of duty: dutifulness to his family, to his friends, to his country, perhaps to his god, and to himself. In his duty to himself he must accomplish what he must, and this may sometimes be one detailed task after another. Thus, he may develop a "workaholic" quality to his life, always seemingly busy and always late. He may be a contemplative procrastinator. He is, therefore, punctilious but not necessarily punctual.

He is almost universally liked, or regarded to be a quiet person who is benignly tolerated. In American parlance, he is often a "nice guy" or a "fine gal". He may be somewhat prudish or even pious. He seems to be rather aloof, ignoring others in a benign way as he quietly goes about his business of pursuits for his own self-satisfaction. However, he is easily approachable and almost always tries to be helpful. He may present himself as a straightforward, uncomplicated person, even a "Simple Simon", but this is misleading and it is only on closer examination that we see the stringent demands that he places on himself.

His natural facial expression is a poker face or deadpan look of perfectionist restraint. As he plays his game of cards, he holds them close to his chest, and he does not particularly wish to discuss how his game is proceeding. In fact, he secretly has everything invested in the finality of success and in the recognition of his success by others. Thus, if recognition does come in any shape or form, whether it is a colleague to bring him good cheer, or actual recognition for something well done in an actual limelight, then he will smile. And his gingival smile, whenever it breaks out through his poker-faced visage, is a sight to behold! It is a warm, radiant, captivating smile, a kind of sheepish smile, appearing suddenly like the sun breaking through the clouds, or of a Cheshire cat suddenly appearing in the mist. It is often so breathtakingly, sincerely radiant that one is led to believe that this smile by itself is enough to give the human race its redeeming social value. And it does not take much insight to realize that this smile is the smile of narcissism bursting forth through the clouds of perfectionism.

As the quiet, somewhat bashful person that he sometimes is, he may surprise others when he mounts the podium as a public speaker. Somewhat stilted at the outset, he slowly gathers momentum and may gradually become radiantly charismatic, especially if he is attempting to persuade his audience.

This individual may have so much pride invested in the recognition of his work as a "conscientious achiever", that embarrassment in the limelight is of special sensitivity to him. In fact, of all the character types, he is the one to blush the most readily. Indeed, in Western society he sometimes has a pinkish or ruddy complexion. If he is male and of the appropriate body habitus, he may have a cherubic, "blushing boy" quality.

He may be quietly ambitious, but lacking qualities of the trait of aggression, this individual is unaggressive and unassertive. He may, in fact, become annoyed when others continually point this out to him. If he is in a position where he should be aggressive, for example as a baseball manager or football coach, he may sometimes adopt a loud voice, but on close inspection he is simply an unaggressive person with a loud voice. Perhaps the most aggressive act of which he is capable is to interrupt someone while he is speaking.

Being unassertive, he finds it difficult to give clear-cut orders. Rather he expects that others will know what to do by his excellent example. He goes forth, and he expects others to follow. But, of course, as they often do not, he may have serious problems maintaining discipline. He cannot berate a subordinate, and he is the master of the short, two-sentence reprimand delivered in an almost apologetic manner.

He does not "play the game" of dominance and submission. His eye contact with others is almost universally good, but does not have the intensity of the NPA+ type. His gestures are reserved, as is his language. Ostentatious behavior is alien to him. His laugh, even if loud, is reserved. His humor has a pleasant impish or elfish quality to it, and he is not the type to play practical jokes of the kind that might cause someone physical discomfort or harm. He enjoys social situations, but is somewhat stilted in demeanor in them.

This usually quiet, unaggressive individual easily bends to the will of others, right? Wrong! He is persistent. He is obstinate. He is recalcitrant. He is downright stubborn! He has a will all of his own, and if he wants to do something in his own orderly way, then wild horses will not be able to budge him from his position.

When criticized he will immediately, quietly, and logically defend his position. If abused, he may scowl, but he may often turn the other cheek, simply not being able to defend himself against aggressive behavior. His only defense may be recalcitrance in the face of the demands of others. He will withdraw himself from the offending individual and ignore him. He will give him "the silent treatment" or pretend not to understand his wishes. He may use various modes of passive resistance, or make lame excuses for his recalcitrance. If pressed further he may quarrel, even vigorously, but he will not fight unless he is cornered. If he does, at long last, punch someone in the nose, it will be in the context of escape or of a narcissistic rage of vanity rather than an aggressive rage of vindictiveness.

He may appear as a somewhat negativistic "passive resister" or "chronic criticizer". If his sense of order is intruded upon repeatedly, he may become more and more negativistic and more and more recalcitrant to the point of resemblance to a PA type. Under greater stress, his negativistic recalcitrance can degenerate either into a catatonic state of near immobility or into a harried nervous state of agitation. In such a latter state he may closely resemble the non-compliant Passive Aggressive NPA− type, or even a hypomanic NA type.

He tends to suffer in silence and to be self-berating. He tends not to be vindictive, neither in a vindictive rage nor in calculated vindictiveness, nor even in frustrating others or begrudging them what is their due. He holds no grudges and sometimes appears to have infinite patience and understanding. He may tease others good-naturedly, even persistently, but this is probably a Western cultural habit, and he is essentially devoid of sadistic trends. If his vanity or his pride in perfection is wounded, then he may respond in a narcissistic "N rage" as has been described earlier.

He is often drawn to activities in which painstaking, repetitive action is required. He may be an artist, a musician, a poet, a craftsman, a collector, or a do-it-yourself tinkerer. He is often the dutiful writer of long, careful letters to his family and he may keep a diary [*11*]].

In the context of mating, the NP type is not aggressive or predatory, although he will certainly acknowledge that he is a sexual being. If he is promiscuous, the overtones of aggression or exploitation are absent. The subjugated love of the aggressive type is unknown to him, as is sadomasochistic sexuality. His love relations are based on his narcissistic and perfectionist qualities: his love is tender rather than unabashedly passionate. He tends not to "fall in love" easily because the decision to devote himself to a mate must be a perfect decision, and like all of his decisions, is not easily made on the spur of the moment. If he enters into a long-term relation with an aggressive-vindictive personage, for example with an NA type, he may suffer in silence like a "brave wife" or a "henpecked husband", all the while berating himself for not being perfect enough to make the relationship an ideal one.

Finally, in his deal with life: "I will be perfect, so life will be perfect to me" he is especially vulnerable to any failure intruding into his existence, whether it be a flat tire on his automobile, a natural disaster or the loss of a loved one. Such failures may register not only as deep disappointments, but as hopeless reversals in what he perceives should be a natural order in life. The loss of a loved one, in particular of a family member, is an incomprehensible, unbearable crushing blow to him. If he does not throw himself on the pyre, then he will enter a melancholic abject state of deep mourning. He will wear black, literally or figuratively, for months or years and often will take his grief to the grave.

His requirements for narcissistic glory, but especially for perfectionist order, may lead him to melancholic depression, which may surprise even those who thought that they knew him well. The news of his circumstances will be met by the stunned disbelief of his neighbors, friends and other family members. They will say, shaking their heads, "We never had the slightest inkling that something was not right... Everything seemed to be in such perfect order..."

In the final analysis, his lack of free will has a touching quality. He may at heart be so innately sympathetic, so intrinsically devoid of evil... so "good", that it is poignant to see him go through life, whatever his real accomplishments, a prisoner of his own demands on himself.

The NP individual has certainly made his mark in history. Both male and female monarchs of the NP type have often emerged as just, strong-willed rulers. However, they sometimes appear as well-meaning "lambs among the wolves" [*12*].

To conclude our discussion, we would refer the reader to Herndon's *Life of Lincoln*: [*13*].

### *From Chapter 11: Disorders of human behavior*

**Personality disorders**

*Obsessive compulsive personality* — Although in reality all of the character types are obsessive and compulsive, we believe that most of the descriptions of the psychiatric literature correspond to our NP type. It is quite humorous that in the old psychiatric literature the NP personage is often referred to as an "anal sadistic" type.

**Autism**

The topic of autism is a complex one. In our book [*14*] we make the point that in Western society, children of the NP personality type with developmental disorders tend to be placed by practitioners into the subjective diagnostic category of "autism" [*15*]. §

[DonkeyHotey]

# 5

# PA type

**"Perfectionistic-aggressive type"**

**Non-sanguine, perfectionistic, aggressive type**

PA types tend to a non-sanguine complexion. Individuals of low temperament can be well-adjusted stodgy, dutiful, socially conscious "solid citizens". Higher temperament individuals can be somewhat stern or haughty extroverts. If they come to absolute power, then more overt sadistic trends may come to the fore. The PA type is relatively uncommon in the USA and Western Europe but common in the Middle East, the Balkans, Eastern Europe and Western Russia.

**Phenotype:** PA

**Genetics:** based on P trait and non-sanguinity (lack if N trait), both being Mendelian dominant

**Animal Model:** baboon

**Inheritance Pattern:** PA types must have at least one parent who is either an A or a PA type.

**Infertility:** Increased probability of miscarriages and stillbirths when mated with either an N or an NP type.

**Rage:** Aggressive-vindictive "A rage" (mass discharge of sympathetic nervous system).

**Also known as:** Reserved aggressive personality. Austere melancholic or paranoid personality. Pseudo-narcissistic extrovert. "The sardonic wit". "The suspicious manipulator". "The Power behind the throne". "The brooding non-sanguine autocrat".

**Complexion:** Non-sanguine. Tending toward sallow, pallid or milky white in individuals with light skin color. Does not blush easily.

**Smile:** Non-symmetric grin or grimace. Mona Lisa "smile". Sardonic smirk. Frozen, toothy but non-gingival grin. Half-open mouthed grin. Grin with short repetitive laugh.

**Photograph:** Usually looks at camera. May pompously look away from camera. Not relaxed. No smile, half smile, tight-lipped sardonic smile, non-symmetric grin or grimace. Non-gingival "frozen smile" showing teeth. Laughs or tries to laugh, showing expressive extroverted countenance.

**Voice:** Confident, contentious, measured, dispassionate.

**Gestures:** Upraised clenched fist, the haughtily cocked jaw, the furrowed brow, the strained tight-lipped mouth and the intimidating glare.

**Handwriting:** Variable. Usually perfectionistic in female. Often slurred or bold illegible scrawl in males. Sometimes messy corrections. Sometimes bold flourishes.

**Sexuality:** Tendency to promiscuity: moderate. Tendency to LGBT in sexual orientation: moderate.

**Color preference:** Muted, blue, dark or white. Conservative, even drab color choices. Active disdain for red, bright colors and multicolors.

**Population genetics:** "The Authoritarian Habitancy", having a high prevalence of PA types, moderate prevalence of A and NPA types, and few N and NP types. Examples: Eastern Europe, Western Russia, Balkans.

**Susceptibilities:** Obsessive paranoia. Pathological "Power behind the throne". Paranoid personality disorder. Covert sadism. Sadomasochistic "morbid dependency" as the dominant or dependent partner.

**Pitfalls:** High temperament PA types can mimic non-sanguine A types, or even zany NA types. Disciplinarian NP types can resemble PA types. Unusual adornment may lead to mistaken conclusion of the N trait (pseudo-narcissism).

### From Chapter 5: A model of human behavior

Here we have an individual who attempts to streamline both his aggressive and perfectionistic qualities into a cohesive unity. How can he possibly do this? His aggressive behavioral trait tells him to forge ahead, to gain power over all others, to achieve vindictive triumph after triumph, to intimidate, and to be first. However, from the trait of perfectionism comes the subliminal voice, "Do it carefully, slowly, perfectly." Thus, perfectionism pacifies aggression, and here we realize that we have discovered the "passive-aggressive" personality of the psychiatric literature. However, this character is not so much passive-aggressive as perfectionist-aggressive.

In a life situation where he has attained a relative equilibrium, or has achieved success in circumstances where he is not threatened, this type may appear as a quiet or fairly outgoing, well-mannered, somewhat stern individual. He may, like all other types, go through life uneventfully, although his relationships with others may be rather tenuous and distant. He may appear as a relatively content, careful, reliable worker who is persistent and pays attention to detail.

This individual, despite his basic passive-aggressive tendencies, may feel a strong need to interact with people, according to the dictates of the gregariousness that modern society demands of him. He may find himself, in fact, in a life situation where he is constantly interacting with others in more or less stressful circumstances. He may then appear in one of two different forms. In one form, he is an individual who sees himself as a perfectionist worker, but whose aspirations are constantly being thwarted by the imperfections or malevolence of others. He, thus, becomes the "chronic complainer" or "chronic criticizer". In a second form, he appears as a fairly gregarious individual with a cutting, sarcastic sense of humor: the "sardonic wit".

If this individual aspires to high ambition, his lack of the N trait means that his ambition must be vested entirely in his aggressive drive. Since his perfectionist trait does not permit the overt use of force, he must use it quietly, unobtrusively, insidiously, obstructively. To a casual observer it may not be noticeably visible. He becomes a manipulator, quietly accumulating relevant information, pondering over it, collating it, putting it into place, using it for insidious, obstructive attacks on others and using it to batten his defensive perimeter. As he becomes manipulative, he becomes more and more mistrustful of others, including his superiors, his colleagues and his subordinates. And in the general mistrust of others he becomes suspicious, cynical and paranoid. Hence, we believe that any study of the paranoid personality type might begin with the study of this character structure.

Continuing with a poorly adjusted individual who has developed a sense of motivation, what emerges is a moody, brooding character who isolates himself within his self-created magic circle of manipulation, suspicion, cynicism and paranoia. And whatever power he attains, and whatever recognition he actually receives from others, do not mask the fact that he is essentially a loner. If circumstances of life allow him to become a political or military strategist, a concentration camp director, a prison guard, a lieutenant in charge of a group of civilians, or a world leader with a nuclear trigger within the reach of his finger, then the road that he paves may lead directly to hell. To the extent that such an individual considers himself above others, he becomes their master and they become his slaves without rights. And since we gradually come to the realization that the A trait of aggression is the root of sadistic acts in man, in a master-slave situation, we gradually realize that the perfectionist-aggressive individual in a position of power has all the potential for becoming a perfectionist-sadist, whether his acts be directed at a single person, ten million people, or an entire ethnic group.

Here we discover an important facet of sadism in man. Diffusely directed aggressive activities whose aim is, to subjugate people into submission and to cause them physical or psychic pain is rooted not only in the open aggression of A, NA, or NPA types, but also in the perfectionist aggression of a PA type. Thus, we might ask ourselves if the danger to the world lies not so much in an arrogant steamroller as in a cynical, brooding loner. It should not escape us that here we have identified a personality type of another tyrannical despot who has throughout history caused the deaths of countless innocent people. And we must examine whether he is inherently a self-destructive type.

No less harrowing, on a smaller scale, is a PA individual who has been subjected to unfortunate circumstances during his years of nurturing and growth, and finds himself a suspicious loner at maturity. One of his inner voices is telling him, "Be strong. Be powerful. Achieve triumph over others." Another voice is telling him, "Direct your efforts. Choose carefully. Do it slowly, perfectly, over and over again until it is just right." It does not take much imagination to surmise that here we have identified one type of a ritualistic criminal, the quiet individual who chooses his victims carefully and is driven to perpetrate a series of stereotyped criminal acts. This is an individual who cannot, of course, show remorse. He is, in fact, following the inner dictates of his very soul.

The reader will appreciate that the implications of sadistic trends in the human character are of utmost importance. Chapter 8 [*16*] considers this topic in detail.

The PA character structure, we propose, may also be the source of other "character disorders" that have been described by psychiatrists. First, it is probable that the condition known as *folie à deux* is based on the symbiotic involvement of two individuals having the PA character structure. This condition is a psychotic disorder in which two schizoid persons, usually members of the same family, mutually share similar paranoid delusions. Second, it is probable that many litigious individuals described under the old category of *compensation neuroses* are of the PA character type.

On a personal level, the PA type, of course, "plays the game" of dominance and submission, becomes involved in subjugation dependencies, and is subject to incitement from a quiet state to the perfectionist-aggressive rage. This begins as a period of outwardly directed seething, and then with the slightest provocation bursts into a directed aggressive-vindictive "A rage".

When dominated, this individual enters a subdued PA− state of perfectionistic schizoid behavior, since he would thereby lack any fully expressed component of sociability or ambition. Thus, he must attempt at all costs to maintain a position of dominance. If, however, he is dislodged from his position, and hopelessness sets in, then he is subject to a deep abject state of schizoid depression.

The PA type can be a member of an interesting symbiotic relationship, called "the power behind the throne".

### From Chapter 6: Character caricatures

As with all the character types, the PA type includes a wide spectrum of individuals who may be enormously successful, and greatly admired, in their societies.

With regard to the physiognomy of the PA individual, his complexion tends to be dull rather than sanguine. It is often swarthy, pale, pallid, dusky or sallow. In a fair individual it may be milky white. His countenance is usually one of a deadpan poker face. In his choice of dress and cosmetics he tends not to adorn himself in an outlandish manner. He may present himself as a "strong silent type", exhibiting courteous reserved charm and well-mannered gallantry. Thus, in unstressed circumstances he may have the quiet personal magnetism of the NP type. He may be greatly admired for his proud bearing, his undemonstrative low-key manner, and his dry humor, often providing others a welcome relief from the madding hysteria of modern society.

The individual of this character type may present himself as something of a high-strung extrovert. More often than not, he tends to keep to himself and may lead a fairly quiet life as a somewhat wary, withdrawn but coolly efficient perfectionist achiever. But with his aggressive drive frustrated to a muted level by the trait of perfectionism, what may emerge is a laconic individual who displays an imperfectly concealed deep dissatisfaction with life. This will not go unnoticed, and his acquaintances will sometimes accuse him, behind his back, of having an air of haughty superiority.

If this individual is constantly interacting with others in a fairly competitive or stressful setting, he may become the classic "passive-aggressive" obstructionist personality, who will not accede to the desires of others except in the most grudging manner. If he is a bit more of an extrovert, then he too may appear as a "chronic complainer" or "chronic criticizer".

Alternatively, this moody personage may find that an effective link with humanity can be made only through the medium of dry humor. In this case, he appears in public as something of a gregarious individual who relies, compulsively and almost exclusively, on his "sardonic wit" to gain the favor of others. Such an individual may display a real talent for creative, albeit sarcastic, humor, and he may be immensely popular with his colleagues for this quality.

In the description that follows, we will present a caricature of one particular PA subtype when he is thrown into the throes of a stressful competitive society, into a position of leadership, or when he is involved in a love relationship.

When this individual is encountered in a stressful setting, one finds oneself picturing him alternately as either an introvert or extrovert. Basically, he appears as a moody extrovert in whom one senses an undercurrent of deep hostility toward the outside world.

He tends to isolate himself, to be introspective and to be basically unfriendly. He is usually coldly calm, but when he is involved in a stressful ambitious venture, a directed task, or a situation of conflict with people, he may become mildly or severely agitated. His pallid face will blanch even more. His normally even voice will rise and have a cutting quality to it. It may barely hide a snarl. His eyes will flash and his brow will furrow. And in his voice one senses not only anger, but also the contempt and disdain of others, and a thinly veiled threat of vindictiveness.

His face in calmer circumstances usually shows the deadpan look of an austere poker-faced perfectionist. Although he is usually at ease before a group of people, to the extent that he believes that he dominates over them, he does not smile easily. What usually emerges is an odd grimace or a grin. He is usually aware of the fact that he cannot at will break out into a natural smile, and in compensation he has developed a short, repetitive laugh accompanied by a closed or half-open mouthed grin, which for him takes the place of the smile that his modern society demands of him. If he tries to smile for a photograph, the result is usually a broad "false smile", a non-symmetric frozen grin, or a sardonic smirk, and often he will not even try.

His handwriting may reflect either his perfectionist or aggressive tendencies. The handwriting may be neat and well formed, especially in the female. In contrast, it may be a slurred illegible scrawl, signifying at the same time his instincts of repressed physical aggression and his disdain for others.

In relations with people he pictures himself as a superior person and would not see himself as isolated. However, his view of life may be seen by his usual physical posture, which is sometimes slightly stooped, with the head dropped slightly down and his eyes directed to the ground before him. He may have, in fact, an amazing capacity to ignore people around him in familiar surroundings, almost to the point of obliviousness. When encountering a subordinate, or in a social setting, his normally stooped posture may change to one of erect, pompous rigidity. His basic unfriendliness may be reflected in obligatory but only cursory greetings to acquaintances or colleagues.

In a stressful social situation where strangers are present he gives the impression of being decidedly uncomfortable and will adopt either a posture of defensive rigidity or will be somewhat agitated. When meeting people in public, he has the roving eyes of suspiciousness, as if scanning the horizon for the possible approach of enemy aircraft. He instinctively evaluates a new arrival for his strengths and weaknesses, as his eyes move in frequent saccades of critical examination. What he is looking for, of course, is the new arrival's particular weakness, his soft underbelly, for in his isolation he senses himself vulnerable, and the only way to conquer his vulnerability is to dominate all others and to be stronger than them.

To the extent that he feels above his fellow humans, he does not make good eye contact with them. If challenged, however, he is the master of staring down his opponent to submission with a steely-eyed intimidating glare or glower. It is a glower that says, "You had better do what I, the perfectionist, expect, or else my vindictive rage may be activated with a hair trigger." His general demeanor, then, may be austere and dour, and may have a sinister aspect to it. His lips may take the form of a fixed smirk. He is the past master of the short derisive laugh.

Is he sarcastic and pessimistic? Yes, he certainly is. But he may be more than that. He may be deeply cynical, and one senses that behind the cynicism of the disasters to come lies the wish for a self-fulfilling prophecy. And in his cynicism and his brooding nature, which exudes the gloom of the basic hopelessness of the human condition, we find the roots of his defensive paranoia and his offensive sadistic potential.

In a position of power, being aloof and suspicious, he is almost unapproachable to his subordinates or colleagues. His door is usually closed, and telephone calls are made in an atmosphere of secretiveness and suspicion. To the extent that he is secretive and mistrustful of others, so are others mistrustful of him. And if they do not trust him, they are intimidated by him, and they are ill at ease with him.

He is an individual who is above all self-righteous, and absolutely convinced that his position of dominance over others is not only right, but inevitable. He may develop a sense of invulnerability. When the going gets tough, and the weaklings scatter in all directions, he will stand firm, tall and proud, with his back to the wall if necessary, and he will survive over, nay conquer, all of his adversaries.

Is he a perfectionist? Yes, he certainly is. He has a sense of duty, but he lacks a broader sense of devotion to others that is often present in the NP and NPA types. His perfectionism lies in the area of pacifying his aggressive tendencies, so that they operate smoothly with maximum efficiency, which means that they are insidious and almost unseen. His *modus operandi* may be summarized by the expression "manipulation with care".

As he discovers, consciously or unconsciously, that his relationships with people are distant, he may attempt to invert his aloofness from time to time. As a perfectionist, an inner voice tells him that he should be warm, loving, sympathetic and gregarious. He will, then, from time to time descend to the level of the lower minions to mingle with his subordinates and colleagues, banter with them, "smile" with them, and attempt to prove to them, and to himself, that at the core he is a down-to-earth humane person. And he must, almost invariably, have at least one "exception that proves the rule" in a cause, or in a person to whom he shows, openly, care and devotion.

He, of course, "plays the game" of dominance and submission, and here we will only briefly mention the implications of this tendency rooted in his aggressive drives. If he is subjugated in marriage or in a love relationship, then he may find himself in a helpless schizoid state and may be reduced to achieving dominance only in occasional vindictive rages. In the dominant role he is, of course, much more successful, provided that his partner is not completely helpless or too tolerant of abuse. Finally, his love relationship may assume a stable symbiotic form in which he adopts the role of what we call the "power behind the throne". As the "power" he protects his mate, who is his sole source of security in life, with all the perfectionist-aggressive talent that his personality type can muster. This type of relationship, the dynamics of which are not consciously perceived by either individual, will be discussed in greater detail below.

The possibility of harrowing sadistic behavior by a PA type has been mentioned previously and will be considered further in Chapter 8 [*16*]. It goes without saying that a motivated PA type is no less committed to success in life through the vindictive triumph over others than is the aggressive A type. The difference lies in the muted way that he goes about it: by manipulation, by conniving, by holding grudges, by begrudging others amenities that they desire or recognition that they deserve, by withholding information from them, and in short, by an always ongoing process of perfecting a multitude of interrelated offensive and defensive actions, so that the final result is a fine tapestry of interwoven vindictive triumphs.

As is the case with all of the personages, this type is one who arouses pathos, for he too is a prisoner of his character structure. He is a prisoner of his aggressive tendencies, for if they were to be suppressed he would be left with only an aimless perfectionistic drive, with no ambition to perfect, and he would thus become schizoid and immobile.

In Maugham's novel *Christmas Holiday* we find a masterful characterization of a non-sanguine type. In the story Simon is a young reporter who dreams of revolution and of becoming the head of a Gestapo-like police force. Charley is his former school companion [17].

### From Chapter 9: Interactions between character types [23]

### The Power behind the throne

The "power behind the throne" is a symbiotic relationship between a perfectionist-aggressive PA type, who plays the role of the Power and another individual, who plays the role of the Throne.

The Throne will often be a trusting, dutiful, ingenuous, perhaps somewhat naive person, who will remain oblivious to the manipulative machinations of the Power. Since the Throne holds the key to success in life, whether it be fortune or fame, he is most likely to be one of the Dominant personages.

It may not be obvious at first who plays the role of dominance in a power-throne relationship, but the Power is actually the dominant individual.

The Power, whatever may be his actual station in life, is deeply insecure. He fears the outside world and is suspicious of it. Indeed he lacks, or senses that he lacks, the natural abilities to become the dominant leader in his competitive society that his character structure demands of him. And in his insecurity he seeks shelter and safety in devoting himself to the Throne. The Power is usually a lonely, somewhat brooding individual, whose few friends fit the "exception that proves the rule" criterion. In fact, the Power's sole bridge to humanity, his sole "exception that proves the rule" may be the Throne.

Somewhat paradoxically, it is in his weakness that the Power mounts to the Throne and takes command in his insidious and barely obtrusive manner. But despite the fact that the Power's security in life is totally dependent on the Throne, it is the Power who is in command. Indeed, the Throne may be subjugated in the dynamics of a morbid dependency (see Appendix B).

How do the Power and Throne perceive the relationship? We need to consider two situations of a power-throne relationship, namely in a *career setting* and in a *love relationship.* In both situations, but especially in a love relationship, the dynamics underlying the relationship are usually not in the slightest recognized by the individuals involved. In a career setting, perspicacious outsiders often have some grasp of the machinations of the Power behind the scenes, but the kindly king sees only a devoted companion, colleague or mate.

In a *career setting* we see a PA individual, often unmarried, who devotes himself to his boss. The devotion appears to be beyond the call of duty. The Power seems to neglect his personal life in his unceasing attention to the Throne. He does, in fact, seek to make the Throne dependent on him; he seeks to enslave him. He does this in various insidious ways, but the most notable way of establishing dominance is by being the holder of all key information. Thus, whatever be the matter at hand, it is the Power who holds the data, the flow sheets, the minutes of prior meetings, the schedules, and so on. Although others may have access to a portion of the key information, no one else, including the Throne, has access to all of it. In fact, the perfectionistic abilities of the Power make him quite adept at juggling times, persons, places and things so that others may not even attempt to challenge him on any point of information. Thus, at the same time that the Power establishes his indispensability, he also maintains his station in life behind a secure defensive perimeter.

The Throne sees only a super-devoted colleague willing to occupy himself with all of those picayune, unpleasant details of running the show. He truly sees the Power as indispensable, so he does not see his manipulative tactics.

Others may notice very little unusual — until they try to make direct contact with the Boss. In that case, they notice that the Power is hovering about, and indeed they may find it impossible to approach the Throne without being confronted by the Power. In fact, the Power lives in secret fear that someone will gain the confidence of the Throne, will bypass the Power, and steal his influence. Any friend of the Throne thereby becomes an enemy of the Power, and the Power will instinctively mobilize all the capabilities available to a perfectionist-aggressive personage to repel the intruder. The attack on the intruder takes on two separate aspects, and is unrelenting until the threat disappears.

First, the Power seizes on some flaw in the intruder, be it in his character, in his philosophy of life or religion, in his personal life, or perhaps on some transgression that he committed in the past. This becomes the basis for unremitting disparagement of the individual, such that the Throne is discouraged from attaining any close personal relationship with the intruder.

Second, when the intruder himself appears on the scene, he may encounter any or all of the techniques of overt or covert aggressive-sadistic activity that we outlined in the Chapter 8 [*16*]. Indeed, very little effort may be required on the part of the Power. The intruder may encounter an icy glare from the Power, and simply feel himself unwelcome. If this is not sufficient, the Power will obstruct, embarrass and insidiously humiliate the intruder before others. As we have mentioned, the PA type has an uncanny ability to spot vulnerabilities in others. In short, the Power has an almost unlimited range of vindictive tactics, and it is not very long before the intruder senses himself so unwanted that he abandons any hope of close personal contact with the Throne. This type of protective vindictiveness may be very effective, and the Throne may find himself rather isolated. He may recognize this fact but may accept it as a necessary fact of life to make the business at hand run so well.

There is a final important point in the dynamics of the "power behind the throne". The Power, being so dependent on the Throne as his solution to life, must continually prove to himself and to others his indispensability. If the Throne becomes *too* successful, therefore, the Power's influence may begin to fade. Thus, the Power secretly, insidiously, and mostly subconsciously seeks to keep the Throne in a relative state of weakness. If the Throne is in danger of being toppled, the Power will, of course, mobilize all of his energies to defend him. However, a series of major victories on the part of the Throne may constitute grave threat to the Power, as they may lead to events that he cannot control. Hence, the Power may take on the aspect of a brooding wolf in sheep's clothing. He cannot enjoy life because he is anxious and insecure, and his relations with the Throne may not be all that good because of his unconscious competition with him.

The personality of the Power may puzzle others, since at times he may appear as a moody, laconic introvert and at others he may be a good-natured extrovert. His moods may be apparently inappropriate. When the Throne suffers an embarrassment or moderate setback, the Power will offer him commiseration and sympathy, but his mood may be one of *la belle indifférence.* Inwardly, but in a deeply repressed manner the Power's heart is leaping with glee, as he cackles to himself, "See how indispensable I am. See how you need me!"

Similarly, if the Throne achieves great victories, especially if the Power was not directly involved, the Power will offer him his congratulations but may retire from the scene in a brooding schizoid abject state.

In a *love relationship* the dynamics of the relationship are similar to those just described. With a Dominant N or NPA individual as the Throne, the marital relationship may be a very stable one indeed.

This couple often appears in a real life situation as an inseparable husband-wife team, in which one of the partners is a PA individual. The key word here is *inseparable.* For example, the couple may comprise a sweet, ingenuous celebrity who is teamed with her stern, overprotective manager-husband. The Power, being profoundly insecure in life, would be utterly lost without his mate. He has little in qualities to embark on a successful career of his own, hence his social and financial aspirations stem from the Throne.

Although the relationship is basically a very stable one, and indeed the Throne himself may be deeply devoted to his mate, the Power is in a continual state of anxiety nevertheless. The Power is continually fearful of losing his mate to events that he will not be able to control, hence he will unremittingly attempt to have a complete knowledge of all persons, places, things and events that have even a remote interaction with his mate. He maintains a constant vigilance against any events that may catch him unawares. He screens the friends of the Throne and resents the slightest independence that his mate may show in his relations toward them. Any telephone call is a threat. If the Throne answers the telephone, the Power must know "Who was it?!!" and in the tone of his voice one senses anxiety and desperation. If a friend shows any indication of being able to influence the thinking of the Throne, then this friend is labeled an intruder and will be repelled from the scene by all the overtly and covertly sadistic machinations that the perfectionist-aggressive personality can conjure.

Finally, in a marital situation as well, the Power secretly finds unconscious joy in the frailties and minor failures of his mate. And this cannot help but to accentuate the free-floating anxiety that he intermittently senses but does not succeed in understanding.

Historical examples of the power behind the throne, in the literal sense, are numerous. In the USA at the presidential level, recent variations on the theme have appeared in the form of wives, secretaries of state and vice-presidents.

[DonkeyHotey]

# 6

# NPA type

### "Sanguine-perfectionistic-aggressive type"

NPA types tend to be sanguine-complexioned, overbearing maternalistic or paternalistic extroverts. All three of the NPA traits are present and fully expressed. Exhibitionism and overt narcissism may be tempered by the P trait. The voice is LOUD and the eye contact intense. NPA types tend to be conventional in their dress and behavior. Their greatest vulnerability is the tendency to explosive rages, often followed by forced affability or apologetics. The female is sometimes denigrated as being "masculine".

**Phenotype:** NPA (sometimes denoted *NPA+ type* for clarity)

**Genetics:** based on N and A traits being recessive, with the P trait being Mendelian dominant

**Animal Model:** We posit that chimpanzees are mainly NA and NPA types.

**Inheritance pattern:** Two NPA types can have children of only NPA or NA type.

**Infertility:** No increased probability of miscarriages and stillbirths when mated with any other character type.

**Rage:** Narcissistic "N rage" (florid rage resembling a childish tantrum), or aggressive-vindictive "A rage" (mass discharge of sympathetic nervous system), or combined "NPA rage".

**Also known as:** Explosive personality. Managerial-autocratic personality. "The overbearing achiever". The sanguine autocratic tyrant.

**Complexion:** Tending toward sanguine or flushed in individuals of light skin color, especially when agitated.

**Smile:** Warm paternalistic or maternalistic smile.

**Photograph:** Looks at camera. Relaxed smile.

**Voice:** Very loud, intense, modulated. Non-stop garrulous. Pontificating.

**Gestures:** Active or hyperactive gestures. Intense eye contact with loud, penetrating voice. Often non-seductive body contact in casual social situations.

**Handwriting:** Variable. Often perfectionistic but sometimes grossly illegible.

**Sexuality:** Tendency to promiscuity: low. Tendency to LGBT in sexual orientation: very low.

**Color preference:** Rather conservative in color choice. Disdains the "garish" color choices of the NA type.

**Population genetics:** "The Demonstrative Habitancy", having a high prevalence of NPA and NA types. Examples: Mediterranean subpopulations, Colombia.

**Susceptibilities:** Overbearing need for control. Explosive personality disorder. Megalomania. Narcissistic personality disorder (NPD).

**Pitfalls:** In absolute power the NPA type can be a cruel disciplinarian, even a tyrant, resembling the behavior of the A type. Hyperactive, high-temperament, promiscuous NPA types can resemble NA types. Loud N or NA types (especially male) can be confused with NPA types. For short intervals the Passive Aggressive NPA− type can mimic the NPA type.

### *From Chapter 5: A model of human behavior*

This individual obviously has a concurrent combination of all three of the NPA behavioral traits: glory, perfection and power. We would expect the following qualities: narcissistic ambition, perfectionistic attention to detail and sense of duty, and the aggressive need for triumph through power. It is not difficult to surmise that this person would be outgoing, active, and vigorous.

This individual, having aggressive qualities, "plays the game" of dominance and submission, splits his personality to a subdued NPA− state when dominated. His love is based on his narcissistic qualities, on the dynamics of the dependency of subjugation, as well as on his sense of perfectionist duty.

This character type would be the most susceptible to be incited to rages, since both his vanity based on narcissism and his pride based on omnipotence are subject to being wounded. This is the narcissistic-perfectionistic-aggressive super-rage, or "NPA rage". This often begins with some violation, reasonable or not, of the individual's sense of perfection, order or justice. That is, all rules should be followed exactly; everything should be exactly in its place. After a few milliseconds of seething, an explosive rage bursts forth, first having an aggressive-vindictive quality to it and being personally directed. Gradually it becomes directed to the horizon, and may finally end as a narcissistic rage of defense and withdrawal. After the rage subsides, this individual's sense of duty may require him to apologize. We believe, in fact, that this individual is the source of the explosive personality disorder of the psychiatric literature, and is described in the writings of Aristotle [18]:

> Quick-tempered people get angry quickly and with the wrong person, or for the wrong reasons, or more than is right. But they soon get over being angry; indeed this is the best point about them. It is because they do not control their anger; they are so quick-tempered that they retort bluntly and then have done...

Finally, we note that here we have found the personality type of the extroverted autocratic tyrant of the historical literature. This imperious personality is known on the one hand for his sense of duty to his people, and on the other hand for his towering rages. Indeed, there is no other character type that comes even close to resembling him. Unfortunately, as we shall see, despite his apparent sense of duty, the NPA autocratic tyrant often finds himself with blood on his hands.

### *From Chapter 6: Character caricatures*

There is no question about it. He is an extrovert. His complexion definitely tends toward the sanguine, especially if he is at all agitated. His voice has an unrestrained quality. It may be forceful. In the female it may have a sharp, piercing quality. His voice may be outright loud, even if he consciously tries not to be overbearing, which often he is. His voice may be very, very LOUD. It may be stentorian, especially in the male, and he may sometimes be heard at the far end of a railway car. It is a voice that seems to long for diffuse dissemination, as he speaks at and through his partner in conversation. It is a voice of narcissism ("how grand I am") and of aggression ("all of you had better listen to what I am saying"). Often he can be identified immediately by his forceful voice alone.

This individual is not relaxed. He radiates a certain intensity and activity, and like the NA type, he too may have difficulty keeping still. In manner, he may be only moderately outgoing, especially if he is in circumstances where he is chronically dominated by stronger individuals. On the other hand, he may be intensely outgoing, affably ebullient or outright truculent. If he is only moderately intense, he has a certain amount of real charm, but often he is so frankly overbearing that his charm is lost in his abrasiveness. He is never at a loss for words. At times he may talk, and talk... and talk. And in his garrulity his smile and laughter may take on a forced intensity.

He has a moderate gait and carries himself with relative confidence. This individual seems to be going somewhere. He usually makes intense eye contact with his partner in conversation, whether the latter be strong or weak, important or unimportant. His prominent eyes have a spirited look about them and may seem to sparkle or even protrude.

In the mature adult, he has a non-seductive maternalistic or paternalistic character, even if he is promiscuous. In the female, she has more of a "wholesome" than a "sexy" demeanor. If her voice is very forceful, her detractors will say that she is "not feminine," "brassy" or even "masculine".

He is reliable, dependable and responsible. He is faithful to his family and friends. If he has children, he has affectionate pride in them and talks about them. He is a "solid citizen". He has a sense of duty to his profession, his colleagues, his business, perhaps his church, and his country. He tends to have a sense of citizenship, of attachments, and of devotion to some ideals. He is, shall we say… rather conventional.

He is expansive, something of a perfectionist and a "doer". His perfectionist tendencies are not as constraining as in the NP type, and he actually gets things done. He likes to get the present job finished and move on to the next task, and he may be a true "workaholic", with his time filled with real activities. Although he may be a procrastinator, he dislikes intensely any ambiguous situations, incomplete information, work half-finished, or any feeling of "loose strings hanging". He tends to be impatient and sometimes impetuous. He cannot bear to stand and watch someone doing something slowly or fumbling about, and will immediately say, "Here, let me do it for you."

We usually see in him a person who is cordial, but who has an air of self-importance. And it is in this feeling of self-importance that there may emerge a barely concealed attitude of callousness, for example in being late for appointments or in downgrading the wishes and aspirations of others.

His gestures are expansive. He may have friendly body contact with his colleagues and acquaintances, but in contrast to that of the NA type, it is of a non-seductive nature. His clothes are usually fitting for the occasion, but he is not one to devote himself to superficial fads or fashions. In the male, especially, his shoes will be polished and his hair combed, but his clothes may even be somewhat ill-fitting. He is, thus, more properly dressed than truly fashionably or gaudily dressed. To the extent that narcissistic-perfectionist tendencies predominate, which is often the case, he will make an effort to have clear, legible handwriting, even when he is in a hurry.

In social situations, he may be at his best. He is the classic after-dinner speaker. He may be a master of inverted modesty in speaking before an audience (e.g., "*He* is an absolutely fantastic person"). He indulges in "hail-fellow-well-met". At a social function he may bellow across the crowded room to welcome a prestigious individual when the latter arrives. He is sympathetic at the core, from his sense of duty, but does not tend to spout forth spontaneous sentimental affection.

If someone does not uphold his standards of perfection, then he will become indignant. He will spread his arms at the sides, with the palms up, in that characteristic stance of perfectionist incredulity. "How could you let that happen? Didn't you realize that...? What is going on here?" If criticized, he will respond immediately and arrogantly in defense, with no prior reflection on the merits of the criticism, like a porcupine bristling its quills. If angered, he becomes sarcastic and ill-mannered; he becomes rude and he shouts. He may become involved in shouting matches, or even fisticuffs, in public with strangers. And if his pride or vanity is trampled upon, he may be incited to the narcissistic-perfectionistic-aggressive blind NPA super-rage, which has been described earlier. The intensity of this red-faced rage may shock others seeing it for the first time. Many NPA individuals are intensely aware of this tendency and consciously attempt to keep a tight lid on their emotions, so that in fact the rage appears only infrequently [*19*].

If an NPA individual is subjugated in a long-term relationship with a companion or mate, and in particular by a "power behind the throne", then for much of his daily life his aggressive component will be strongly muted. He may thus appear as an individual somewhat placidly riding the merry-go-round of life, apparently little motivated and somehow "lacking in ambition".

Moving on to an NPA individual who is overtly power-seeking, he is sometimes grandiloquent, and he may lose all sense of propriety. One senses that he is often making a conscious effort to be not overly overbearing or too dominating. He assumes leadership because he thinks — nay he knows — that he is the best one for the job. But despite his efforts to convince others and himself that he is not aggressive in a cutthroat manner, he has a pervasive inward feeling that no one should push him around and that he should attain heights of excellence — that he should succeed to the very limits of his ambition. As in other aggressive types, but in a form muted by his sense of duty, there emerges the deep conviction that he should be above the masses and above the competition. It is a conviction fed by narcissistic ambition acting synergistically with his innate aggressive drive, with both being forged and tempered by the behavioral complex of perfectionism.

If he aspires to be "the boss", then the boss he is — there is no question about it — and his sense of restraint may fade. He may reveal a barely camouflaged arrogance. He then requires that his instinct for perfectionism be fulfilled. He requires that others pay constant attention to the details that his sense of "doing things well" requires. He demands "spit and polish". He insists on punctuality. He requires the continual approbation of his colleagues but would be embarrassed by their overt adulation.

He will dominate the conversation in a group. He tends to speak compulsively at conferences. If a difference of opinion arises, he will become agitated and will feel that he must have the last word.

He has pride in his honesty. Overt prevarication is anathema to him. However, to maintain his position of dominance, which he somehow feels in his bones is a right granted to him directly from the heavens, he will have no compunction with regard to the withholding of information that his opponents might use against him.

If he is not so much a boss than an upcoming achiever, for example in a hierarchal structure, then he becomes an "expert" in some field. Once his area of expertise is established it tends to expand in two ways. First, it expands in his own mind so that he becomes an expert not just in his narrow field but in the broader areas of technology, science, education or philosophy. Second, it becomes, by his own word of mouth, disseminated in time and space: everyone should have the benefit of his expertise.

Despite his often overbearing demeanor he has pride in his manners, in decorum, and he rarely would insult an individual to his face. Vindictiveness toward others and sadistic behavior may be overt, it is true, but usually it is well camouflaged and only subtly present. It may take the form of apparently good-natured but persistent teasing of a subordinate or opponent, being condescending toward him, overpowering him in public under a mass of sarcastic verbiage, or in that passive vindictive triumph that has been classic since time immemorial, simply leaving without saying good-bye.

As a leader or as a head of the family, he becomes an autocrat and cannot tolerate insubordination. He is the classic martinet with panache. The slightest indication of disloyalty may be dealt with unbounded harshness, and no punishment, even corporal punishment, will be excessive. Family members will not be exempt. Although others may stand aghast at the intensity of his vengeance, to his own mind he is a misunderstood man of mercy whose hand is occasionally forced to mete out harsh justice. In such circumstances his only saving grace is that he tends to mellow with age.

As an aggressive type, the NPA individual certainly "plays the game" of dominance and submission, but the "game" is often muted by his sense of duty. His aggressive tendencies are moderated by the behavioral complex of perfectionism, but in the framework of narcissistic behavior, the resultant character structure is very different from that of the PA type. In marriage he will usually be a devoted and faithful to his mate. But if the relationship goes awry, he will become a somewhat passive "situational sadist" and may finally attempt to extricate himself. He may be sexually promiscuous. In other words, his sense of duty has limits.

Finally, like his cousin the NP type, he too has made a "deal with life", though in muted form. If he takes care of the business of life, then the business of life should take care of him. And if it does not, then life's failures are taken very, very hard, subjecting this active, vigorous individual to the depths of an abject state. When he falls, it is all the more painful, because it is, in his own mind, the mighty who has fallen.

In the final analysis, this individual, too, is a prisoner of his character structure, and he is puzzled by the demons that seem to be driving him in three different directions. His life may be one of constant turbulence as he tries to streamline his narcissistic, perfectionistic and aggressive traits into a cohesive unity, all the while trying to keep a lid on his NPA super-rage. And it is only in looking into his character structure that he may begin to create for himself a life situation that is compatible with psychic survival in his human society.

# 7

# NPA= type

### "Perfectionistic compliant type"

Passive Aggressive types are those who have the A trait of aggression, but it is partially inhibited by genetic and/or environmental factors. *Compliant* Passive Aggressive types are those in whom the A trait is profoundly inhibited (notation A=). *Non-compliant* Passive Aggressive types are those in whom the A trait is partially, but not profoundly, inhibited (notation A−).

In compliant types the trait A is profoundly suppressed, so that whatever the circumstances they tend not exhibit aggressive behavior in social situations. They can exhibit the aggressive "A rage", but this is unusual. Compliant types tend to be introverted and may seek a life style involving little responsibility and much protection. Sexually promiscuous individuals are vulnerable to abusive relationships and may have a tendency to masochistic behavior.

**Phenotype:** NPA=

**Genetics:** The underlying genetic structure is the same as for the NPA Dominant type, except that in addition the A trait is modulated by genetic and/or environmental factors.

**Rage:** "N rage", "A rage" or combined "NA rage". In most compliant individuals the rages are rarely seen.

**Also known as:** "NP like" compliant. Quiet achiever Passive Aggressive. Depressive, masochistic personality. Submissive, dependent or self-effacing personality. "The shrinking violet".

**Complexion:** Tending toward sanguine or flushed in individuals of light skin color. Blushes very easily with embarrassment.

**Smile:** Warm smile when at ease. Otherwise nervous smile.

**Photograph:** Uncomfortable before camera in unfamiliar settings.

**Voice:** Nervous voice pattern with speech hesitation. Low in intensity.

**Gestures:** Reserved and tentative.

**Handwriting:** Neat and legible, as a slave writing for his masters.

**Sexuality:** Tendency to promiscuity: low. Tendency to LGBT in sexual orientation: moderate.

**Color preference:** Conservative in color choice.

**Population genetics:** "The Introspective Habitancy". See Passive aggressive NPA− type.

**Susceptibilities:** Shyness. Masochism. Sadomasochistic "morbid dependency" as the dependent partner. Social phobia. Panic disorder. Reactive depression. Dependent, avoidant personality disorder. See also Passive Aggressive NPA− type.

**Pitfalls:** NPA= individuals can superficially resemble NP, NPA− or Borderline types.

### *From Chapter 5: A model of human behavior*

This introverted individual carries the mottos, "I am the most unselfish, the most sympathetic and the most loving," or "I will do anything, but anything for you so long as you protect me for the rest of my life."

He has, perhaps without realizing it, lacked aggressive tendencies from early childhood. He may be a self-conscious, painfully shy "shrinking violet" and be easy prey to any aggressive type. He may have a strong feeling, or a vague uncomfortable suspicion, that all was not well during his very early childhood. Somehow, he feels and acts as if, in the deep recesses of his mind, he were ashamed of something that he is, guilty of something that he did wrong or something he should have done right, or was somehow, somewhere deeply humiliated before others.

Being defenseless, and easily frightened, he fears any demands to be made upon him, particularly those forcing him to any position of responsibility. In fact, the words "responsibility", "ambition", "career" or "success" are taboo to him, and may send shivers down his spine. If he finds himself in a hierarchal structure, he wants to stay right where he is. He certainly does not want to move up to a position of greater responsibility, and he will invoke the "Peter Principle" in his defense. That is, he will say that he does not want to exceed the limits of his capabilities, which despite intensive rationalization, must have become painfully obvious to him.

Although his aggressive qualities have been suppressed into profound submission, they are nevertheless latently present. He does "play the game" of dominance and submission, but instinctively feels himself helpless at the bottom of the "pecking order". In his helplessness, his only salvation in life is to offer to all comers helpfulness, love, sympathy, compassion and self-sacrifice.

In love relationships the "shrinking violet" flourishes into a "clinging vine", and he "falls in love" in the form of a morbid dependency with almost any strong individual. And if he obtains a commitment for protection, it must be total. He must have everything done for him, while in return he offers little else than the promise of his total abandon to "true love".

In his insatiable desire to achieve safety in the promises of protection and love, he becomes vulnerable to abuse by others, and in fact, does come to feel that he is abused. He, thus, finds himself in the position of offering himself to be abused in order to fulfill the needs of his character structure and to find satisfaction in his life. Hence, it is in this character structure that we find the roots of *masochism*, that is, the finding of satisfaction in life through being abused by others. He may, in fact, be overtly sexually masochistic.

As with all of the character types, frustration of the most serious kind is engendered when the premises of the underlying character structure are threatened. For this individual, the worst threat is that of the loss of his protective master, boss or subjugator. This will be defended vigorously in the form of a claim of fidelity from the master. Since he, the slave, has been so faithful and loving, the master must respond in turn. The dynamics of such a "morbid dependency" are discussed in more detail in Appendix B.

If frustration mounts to a breaking point, the individual may, finally, incite himself to an aggressive-vindictive rage. This will surely surprise his onlookers, who are used to seeing a very quiet, shy individual. It will also surprise and frighten the individual himself, who may not have known that a spirit of aggression lurked deep in the catacombs of his character.

If the hopelessness of the situation comes to the fore, then a deep abject state of depression will ensue. In this individual, the abject state is characterized by suffering, and the suffering provides a source of "positive feedback" to the unconscious motivations behind his basic character structure. That is, the suffering becomes a further reinforcing alibi for the individual's not mobilizing himself, and for his continuing demand that he be rescued by the master, or by anyone else, without any positive effort at all on his part.

The above descriptions would apply to introspective individuals of the NPA= and NA= types, who would superficially somewhat resemble the NP and N types, respectively. That is, the NPA= type would tend to be a quiet, meticulous perfectionist worker, while the NA= type would tend to be more labile, more aware of his physical and sexual attributes, and less a perfectionist worker than a task-oriented "doer".

## *From Chapter 6: Character caricatures*

This individual's character structure, whatever its resultant complexity and whatever his real accomplishments in life, seems to be constructed around a nidus of a feeling of shame. He is an introvert. He has the so-called "inferiority complex".

He may be blandly passive or a true "shrinking violet". He has a low, restrained voice, and he is not articulate. His countenance suggests a trace of sadness. His movements are tentative and his gestures reserved. His eye contact with others is poor, as he displays the averted eyes of a slave before his masters, which in his case includes almost everyone with whom he comes in contact. He shrinks in the presence of kings, but also in the presence of shopkeepers.

Meeting people in a business or social situation is an ordeal for him. He forgets names as soon as the introductions are uttered. If he is required to make the introductions himself, his mind goes blank and he may enter a state of panic. He is very uncomfortable before a group of strangers. He lives in fear of being called upon to speak extemporaneously. If he must give a speech he will write it out word for word or commit it to memory, fearing that his mind will go blank when it comes time to deliver it. When he does deliver it, his nervousness is apparent, all the more so if his audience is hostile or in the least bit threatening. For the same reason this individual will not be seen on television unless he is accompanied by his master.

He will be uncomfortable and feel anxious if he must go to a social function where strangers will be present. What he fears most is a medium sized group of six to twelve persons, where he might suddenly become the center of attention. Paradoxically, though, he yearns for the presence of others, and to stay home in loneliness is a state of shame that he tries to avoid or hide at all costs.

He has a poor self-image but does not try to bolster it. Even though he may possess the N trait of narcissism, he tends not to adorn himself excessively (but the NA= type may, indeed, adorn himself flamboyantly). His dress is usually reserved and may be outright shabby. In fact, any state of ostentatiousness is alien to him. If he sees himself suddenly in a mirror he may startle himself, and he is not particularly enamored by what he sees. He may at times consciously wish that he were not he, but someone else.

Having renounced competitiveness, he has all of his pride invested in helping others and in trying to please them. He is in his self-effacing way overhelpful, overkind, overcaring and oversympathetic. His handwriting, written as it is for the benefit of others, is nicely legible. And in his pride he sees himself, not as a selfish person whose claim is to be cared for throughout his journey through life, but as a selfless saint who is indispensable to his boss or to his mate and family.

His taboo on competitiveness and on any aspirations for himself pervades his entire life, from his important decisions of how to gain his livelihood and whom to marry, to the less important ones regarding the minutiae of his daily existence. Feeling as he does as a stowaway on the ship of life, he fears that if he does anything implying independence from his protectors then he might suddenly find himself in a lifeboat, alone at sea and having to fend for himself in the struggle for survival in his hostile world.

In space and time, he is something of a lost soul. He may have a magic circle, of ten-mile radius, from which he dare not leave. He may have only the vaguest idea of the locations of nearby states, cities or townships. He may not have the slightest idea where the maze of highways near his home actually leads. If he goes on a trip, he enjoys himself as he is piloted about by his protector, but he will have only the slightest idea in geographical terms where he has been. He is totally incapable of reading maps or transportation schedules, and may ascribe this inability to some kind of learning disability. In fact, if he is not taken somewhere, he would not dream of going alone. Hence, in contrast with the Resigned type whose pride is vested in complete independence, the compliant type has all of his pride invested in complete dependence on his protector, protectors or subjugator [20]. §

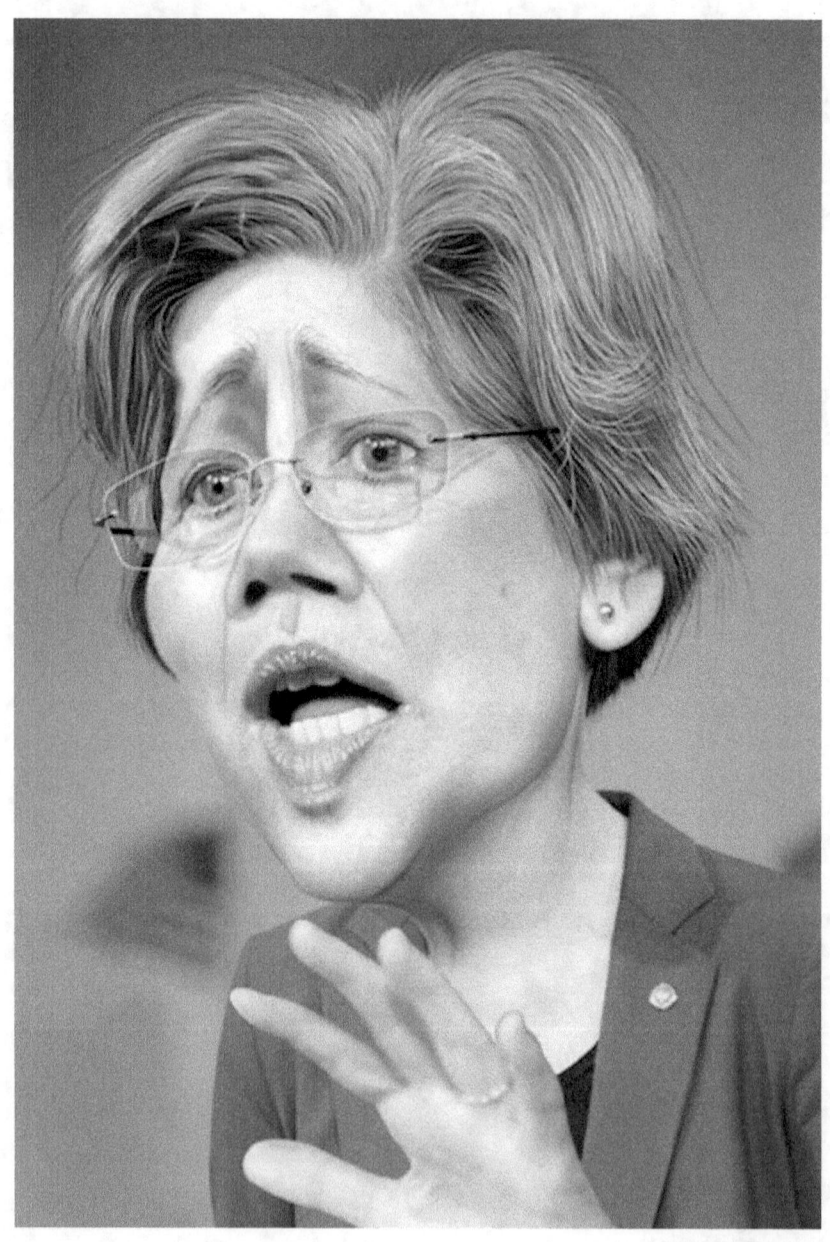

[*DonkeyHotey*]

# 8

# NPA− type

**"Perfectionistic non-compliant type"**

Passive Aggressive types are those who have the A trait of aggression, but it is partially inhibited by genetic and/or environmental factors. *Non-compliant* Passive Aggressive types are those in whom the A trait is partially, but not profoundly, inhibited (notation A−). *Compliant* Passive Aggressive types are those in whom the A trait is profoundly, inhibited (notation A=).

In non-compliant types the trait A is partially suppressed, but depending on the circumstances they can exhibit aggressive behavior in social situations. These individuals tend to be non-confrontational. They can exhibit the aggressive "A rage", but this is unusual. The sanguine N trait may be expressed as "narcissism", but this is very variable. Low-temperament individuals tend to be introverted. Higher temperament individuals can be "nervous extroverts", often with speech hesitancy or tremor.

**Phenotype:** NPA−

**Genetics:** The underlying genetic structure is the same as for the NPA Dominant type, except that in addition the A trait is modulated by genetic and/or environmental factors.

**Rage:** "N rage", "A rage" or combined "NA rage". In most non-compliant individuals the A rage is rarely seen.

**Also known as:** "NP like" non-compliant type. The "passive-aggressive" personality. Agitated achiever submissive. Reactive depressive personality. "Type A" personality.

**Complexion:** Tending toward sanguine or flushed in individuals of light skin color. Blushes easily with embarrassment.

**Smile:** Relaxed social smile rarely seen. Nervous smile.

**Photograph:** Usually uncomfortable before camera, sometimes to the extent of phobia. Mugs for camera.

**Voice:** Nervous voice pattern with speech hesitation. Silent when under stress.

**Gestures:** Agitated, inconsistent and tentative.

**Handwriting:** Usually legible but "jerky" quality, with large variations in size of letters. Sometimes slurred. Sometimes messy corrections.

**Sexuality:** Tendency to promiscuity: moderate. Tendency to LGBT in sexual orientation: moderately high.

**Color preference:** Variable according to the individual and situation, but usually there is a discomfort with bright or ostentatious colors.

**Population genetics:** "The Introspective Habitancy", having a high prevalence of NPA− types, and moderate prevalence of NP and NPA types. Example: Anglo-Saxon subpopulations, Finland.

**Susceptibilities:** Shyness. Public speaking phobia. Social phobia. Avoidant personality disorder. Speech hesitation, stuttering. Panic disorder. Reactive depression. Narcissistic personality disorder (NPD, in dominant role). Sadomasochistic "morbid dependency" as either the dominant or dependent partner. Coronary artery disease ("Type A" personality).

**Pitfalls:** Unstressed NPA− individuals can resemble NP types. High temperament NP types can resemble NPA− types. Sexually profligate Passive Aggressive types can have behavior that could be confused with that of N or NA types. Borderline types can resemble Passive Aggressive types.

### From Chapter 5: A model of human behavior

The character structure of the non-compliant type is similar to that of the compliant type. That is, this individual is not a forceful person and may even be a shy, self-conscious introvert. We noted that the compliant type views his life from the bottom of the "pecking order" and is quite satisfied to stay there, somewhat contentedly awaiting retirement and death, provided that he is well taken care of and protected. However, whereas the non-compliant type also views life from the bottom of the pecking order, he has one eye open toward the top and aspires to achieve power, glory and domination, even if ever so briefly.

He does, in fact, retain his narcissistic behavioral trait, even though his aggressive capacities have been stunted (NPA− and NA− types). He is, therefore, in the constant throes of an intrapsychic conflict. He desires narcissistic glory, but he lacks the aggressive power to support his ambitious drive. In competitive society he may be so unsure of himself, and fraught with stage-fright, that at the same time that he craves the limelight, he also fears it. In overtly stressful circumstances, he begins to glance about in search of protection or escape, like the classic coward who dies a thousand deaths.

He can ascend to an energetic A+ state for only a brief period, and he is quite apprehensive and vulnerable there if he is in competitive surroundings. If he encounters an aggressive type in competition with him while in the energetic state, he becomes agitated, uncomfortable, easily intimidated, and is usually easily defeated. He may find himself behaving like a frightened rabbit. For one so low to have aspired so high, the agony of defeat is severely stressful. Not only does he come crashing down to his original A− state of submissiveness in an abrupt personality split, but he may also enter an abject state of depression because of his failure. With repeated failures, he may become more and more wary of any aggressive ventures, or even of assertive behavior toward others of lower status. He may develop phobias or "panic attacks" with respect to situations in which he has previously felt himself to be humiliated.

Finally, he comes to temper somewhat his desires for glory. He will convince himself that somehow, in this life anyway, he was not meant to accomplish those glorious deeds of his visions. He becomes an opportunist and a dreamer. If opportunity knocks and presents itself to him, with little danger of his being overcome or humiliated in the presence of aggressive types, then he will abruptly split his personality to the energetic state and seize the opportunity by the horns. If he is lucky, he will descend to his baseline submissive state of his own accord, with the victory intact. To this individual "nature abhors a vacuum", and if a vacuum presents itself he will step into the situation. If thrown into a lifeboat with stronger types, he will be quite content to stay submissive. But if the others are weaker, then he will take command, and command he will. In the land of the blind, the one-eyed man is king!

The love relationships of this character type are, as one may have guessed, often based on the "morbid dependency", and he may adopt the role of subjugator or subjugated, or even both simultaneously in a love triangle. Using the most blunt of terminology of psychiatry, he may assume the role of either a hardened sadistic master, or of a suffering masochistic lover desirous of nothing in life except to lose himself completely in a warm, tender, sentimental love of subjugation to another individual.

As with any individual possessing the trait of aggression, if the individual adopts the dominant role in a relationship of subjugation, or to the extent that he comes to consider himself above any person or group of people, then aggressive-sadistic trends may come to the fore. These may show themselves in several ways:

First, the aggressive sadistic behavior may be overt, especially if the individual is incited to one of his rare aggressive-vindictive rages. If goaded into a barroom fight, this type can become a wild panther, and he may not stop until no one is left standing and until every bottle in the barroom is broken.

Second, if the circumstances present themselves, he may become paranoid and quietly manipulative, hence similar in behavior to a PA type.

Third, he may become a "situational sadist" if he is tied to a relationship with a companion or mate from which, because of life circumstances, he cannot extricate himself.

Finally, his ventures to the energetic state of aggression if frequent and short-lived, may become transient states of exhilaration, or thrills.

As may be predicted, NA− and NPA− individuals would have behavioral characteristics somewhat similar to N and NP dominant individuals, respectively. In addition to being incitable to aggressive-vindictive rages, the NA− and NPA− types would also be capable of narcissistic or combined NA rages.

What finally emerges in the non-compliant Passive Aggressive character type is a basically introverted, active, even hyperactive, individual who may be capable of assuming practically any psychic state of any of the other character types. He may be meekly submissive or even masochistic. He can be sadistic. He can go into the wildest of rages and be depressed into the deepest of abject states. He can split his personality to aggressive behavior, and back to the submissive state in a flash. He can see the "morbid dependency" from both ends, even simultaneously. He may go into flurries of introspective narcissistic-perfectionist work activity of the NP type, or of hypersexual activity of the NA+ type. He may feel like an NPA+ king, or he may be drawn by circumstances to the psychopathic aggression of a PA+ individual. He seems to have the widest range of psychic states and the widest range possible of emotions. He has ability to empathize with practically any of the other character types but not necessarily to sympathize with them. That is, he may be to feel what his subjugated partner is feeling, but not necessarily able to offer his love and sympathy to him.

But life goes on, and little by little, the non-compliant type loses his energy and vitality and becomes compliant or resigned. The sweet verve of youth dissipates itself, little by little, and he comes to await the sweet kiss of death.

### *From Chapter 6: Character caricatures*

We focus first on the NPA− type. This individual appears to be an introvert who periodically seems to come out of his shell. His demeanor, in fact, is highly dependent on the circumstances of the moment.

His baseline personality is essentially that of an affable compliant type, and his facial features often show that characteristic trace of sadness. But his car is parked outside, with the engine running, and it may be a sport model capable of flying him to the pinnacles of the glory of his imagination. Thus, this individual has a subtle, or sometimes not so subtle, agitated, fidgeting demeanor, as if he wants to go somewhere. He fidgets with his hair, his hands, his moustache, as if they were masturbatory equivalents suggesting repressed sexual yearnings. In stressful situations his eye contact with others is abysmal, and indeed he often has the wandering eyes of perpetual apprehension. His handwriting often reflects his agitation, and it is often barely legible, with many corrections, or else well-formed but jerky.

He is a compliant type who appears to be highly motivated, and indeed that he is. But more often than not his objectives in life are unclear. He would like desperately to succeed in life, but his ambition lacks the necessary aggressive component, and he would avoid using the word "career". He seems to scrutinize a ship as it passes, and he jumps on it in the hope that it will take him to reasonable success. But he, too, deep in his heart, feels that he is a stowaway on board.

The dynamics of this individual were presented earlier and will not be repeated here in detail. To summarize, he is an opportunist, a dreamer. He is introspective, sometimes a shy individual who requires privacy. He has something of a free spirit, and may be a traveler. He periodically aspires to heights and crashes to depths, like a majestic eagle whose wings have been clipped. He knows the thrills and exhilarations of the conquests of his dominant cousins, but he knows that his successes in the realm of aggressive behavior are of the hit-and-run variety, and that he cannot have aspiration to domination or to effective leadership in a career.

If he does ascend to a position of leadership on the basis of his affability or his intellectual qualities, he does not inspire confidence before his colleagues and subordinates. He is frequently very self-conscious. If at all intimidated, he becomes tongue-tied; his voice loses its forcefulness, and he tends to fidget and to stammer or mumble. Even if he is an expert in his field he cannot mount the podium with any confidence to speak extemporaneously. He exasperates others with his indecisiveness, as he tries to please everyone. He is vulnerable to the views of any strong personality, and as he is at the mercy of the last person with whom he speaks, he may be constantly changing his views. Thus, others will accuse him of being "good-natured" but "weak minded". Often they will misinterpret his apprehensive reticence for cynical indifference. His basic attitude toward life is seen in his usual photograph: he is not comfortable looking at the camera, and often he is not smiling.

In love relations he may assume any role in the "game", and he may lead a rather quiet life, playing either the dominant or submissive role of subjugation. If he is not too shy and is successful in competitive society, he is exceedingly vulnerable to being subjugated by a "power behind the throne". Alternatively, he too may assume the role of a quiet hunter or "bird of prey". In fact, he and the NA type are often both out on the prowl, looking for each other, and when they meet sparks are bound to fly. More often than not, an affair of the "lightning and thunder" variety begins, and exciting and exhilarating as it may appear, it is usually destined to achieve no lasting stability. As has been described earlier, sadomasochistic elements inevitably seep into the relationship, the two partners never really gain an understanding of their own or each other's needs and motivations, and the relationship comes to an end when the NA partner moves on to a new companion to continue the chain reaction.

Finally, we see the frustration that the non-compliant type faces throughout his active life. He has a strong sense of narcissistic ambition but a stunted component of aggression. And during his jerky ride through life he finds that others do not particularly admire his jerkiness, are ill at ease with him, and he often finds himself isolated. Sometimes he, too, seems to be a speedboat out of control in a fogbound harbor, and it is only in looking at his own basic character structure that he can begin to lift the fog and bring himself under control.

Insight into the basic character of non-compliant types may be acquired in the study of the lives of historical figures who have led very full lives, such as Edward VIII, Henrik Ibsen and Somerset Maugham (in particular the self-revealing character of Philip in *Of Human Bondage*). The NPA− type is often attracted to a career in professional writing, and to journalism in particular [*21*]. §

# 9

# NA= & NA− types

**Non-perfectionistic types:**

- **Compliant type, NA=**
- **Non-compliant type, NA−**

Passive Aggressive types are those who have the A trait of aggression, but it is partially inhibited by genetic and/or environmental factors. *Compliant* Passive Aggressive types are those in whom the A trait is profoundly inhibited (notation A=). *Non-compliant* Passive Aggressive types are those in whom the A trait is partially, but not profoundly, inhibited (notation A−).

The NA= and NA− types distinguish themselves from their close cousins, the NPA= and NPA− types, in lacking the P trait of perfectionism. The trait A is partially suppressed, but depending on the circumstances these types can exhibit aggressive behavior in social situations, and they have the capacity to exhibit the aggressive "A rage". Since the P trait is lacking, in NA= and NA− types the sanguine N trait may be overtly expressed as "narcissism", as if these individuals were introverted, submissive or nervous N or NA types.

**Phenotype:** NA= (compliant), NA− (non-compliant)

**Genetics:** The underlying genetic structure is the same as for the NA Dominant type, except that the A trait is modulated by genetic and/or environmental factors.

**Rage:** "N rage", "A rage" or combined "NA rage". In most Passive Aggressive individuals the A rage is rarely seen.

**Also known as:** "N like" Passive Aggressive types.

**Complexion:** Tending toward sanguine or flushed in individuals of light skin color. Blush very easily.

**Smile:** Warm smile when at ease. Otherwise nervous smile.

**Photograph:** Uncomfortable before camera in unfamiliar settings. Mugs for camera.

**Voice:** Nervous voice pattern with speech hesitation.

**Gestures:** More expressive than in perfectionistic Passive Aggressive types.

**Handwriting:** Non-perfectionistic.

**Sexuality:** Tendency to promiscuity and to LGBT in sexual orientation: high (higher than in the perfectionistic Passive Aggressive types).

**Color preference:** Preference for bright and multicolors, akin to the Dominant N and NA types.

**Population genetics:** Similar to the perfectionistic Passive Aggressive types, NPA= and NPA−.

**Susceptibilities:** Similar to the perfectionistic Passive Aggressive types. Bipolar, borderline personality disorder. ADD, Asperger syndrome. Shyness. Public speaking phobia. Social phobia. Speech hesitation, stuttering. Panic disorder. Reactive depression. Narcissistic personality disorder (NPD, in dominant role). Sadomasochistic "morbid dependency" as either the dominant or dependent partner. Eating disorders. Coronary artery disease.

**Pitfalls:** Depending on temperament and other factors, NA= and NA− individuals can superficially resemble the N or NA Dominant types, the NPA= and NPA− Passive Aggressive types, or Borderline types.

### *From Chapter 6: Character caricatures*

We now turn to the NA− type, keeping in mind the three basic attributes that rule his life: unbridled narcissism, non-perfectionism, and submission. In fact, the two traits of unbridled narcissism and submission seem to be continually acting in antagonism in this personage, so that sometimes he appears as an affable extrovert, and sometimes as a submissive introvert. In addition, lack of the behavioral complex of perfectionism often gives his character structure a labile, fragile quality.

Once the character structure of this personage is recognized, one can predict his general behavior, almost as if it were a foregone conclusion. In real life he appears as an affable, sanguine-complexioned, somewhat subdued individual who, despite his generally submissive nature, is ever ready to respond to the call of the limelight. If his life situation supports him so that his unbridled narcissism comes to the fore, then he may be somewhat expansive or even charismatic. He tends to adorn himself or "dress up" − sometimes strikingly − to a much greater extent than his NPA− cousin, and indeed this is often the most obvious superficial difference between these two types. He may, in short, display any of the attributes that we have come to associate with the charming, but often flighty, N character type.

If he trends toward being a Compliant Submissive type, he is exactly that − however much he would like to ignore or deny this facet of his personality. His tendency to be sympathetic and agreeable pervades his daily life, and his acquaintances will invariably consider him to be a "nice person". However, having a remnant of the trait of aggression, he reveals himself to be a "player of the game" of dominance and submission in stressful situations, being susceptible not only to red-faced narcissistic rages but also − albeit rarely − to the aggressive-vindictive rage.

In competitive society his submissive trait sooner or later becomes evident. When challenged, he is easily intimidated, and others will say that "he can't seem to get it all together", or will accuse him of "bumbling" or of "histrionics". If he comes to power on the basis of his narcissistic charisma, at the highest level of society, then he requires much support from his entourage in his attempts to achieve his grandiose visions of unbridled glory. Hence, he is easily subjugated, and indeed, hovering in the wings there is often seen a protective, perfectionist "power behind the throne", always ready to ensure that everything will progress with the precision of a well-oiled machine.

In adolescence the NA− type is an active but reserved individual who will often describe himself as being "on the shy side". Nevertheless, his unbridled narcissism is continually seeking to overcome his submissive shyness, and he may be attracted to expansive, soaring projects, again reminiscent of the activities of the self-flaunting N character type. He may, in fact, be attracted to public speaking, to a career in modeling, to the stage, or to the dance.

If he aspires to be an actor, he may be highly successful in his portrayal of the affable, kind-hearted − but perennially abused hero or heroine. Often, however, he is only moderately successful, since his generally submissive nature continually intrudes into his desire to be the forceful personality of his dreams. Although his likable qualities usually carry the day, onlookers will often titter behind his back for his general lack of talent, for his lack of "substance", and for his penchant for appearing as a second-rate actor in the grade-B motion picture.

Like his cousin the NPA− type, the NA− personage may lead a successful, relatively calm existence if his life situation is well supportive. If it is not, then this labile personality is prone to transient masochistic love affairs, hypochondria, phobias, fugues, panic attacks, agitated reactive depressions, as well as episodes of euphoria and hysteria.

Finally, we note that Passive Aggressive individuals who have the N trait tend to have, even more than their Dominant cousins, a sanguine or flushed complexion. §

*[KDP/Adobe]*

# 10

# NP−A and N−A Types

- **Perfectionistic type, NP−A**
- **Non-perfectionistic type, N−A**

Resigned types are those in whom the trait of aggression is partially suppressed by either genetic and/or environmental factors *after* maturity (notation −A). In Passive Aggressive types the trait of aggression is partially suppressed *before* maturity (notation A− and A= for non-compliant and compliant types, respectively).

In Resigned types the trait A may be suppressed in 1) a former Dominant type, or 2) a former non-compliant Passive Aggressive type. Because of environmental factors, or "stress", the individual becomes detached, or "abdicates", from competitive social interaction in order to devote himself to more serene activities. The sanguine N trait may be expressed as "narcissism", but this would be especially unusual in the NP–A type.

**Phenotype:** NP−A (perfectionistic), N−A (non-perfectionistic)

**Genetics:** Depends on whether the individual was a former NPA/NA Dominant type, or a former NPA−/NA− Passive Aggressive type.

**Rage:** "N rage", "A rage" or combined "NA rage". In most Resigned types the rages are rarely seen.

**Also known as:** Sanguine resigned. Avoidant or detached personality.

**Complexion:** Tending toward sanguine or flushed in individuals of light skin color, especially in former Passive Aggressive types.

**Smile:** Former NPA and NA types: smiles easily. Former Passive Aggressive types: relaxed social smile rarely seen.

**Photograph:** Former NPA and NA types: relaxed. Former Passive Aggressive types: camera-shy.

**Voice:** Depends on former NPA type.

**Gestures:** Reserved.

**Handwriting:** Usually neat and legible.

**Sexuality:** Variable according to life situation. Wary of strong attachments.

**Color preference:** Variable according to the individual and situation, but usually there is a discomfort with bright or ostentatious colors.

**Population genetics:** Etiology of Resigned types is highly dependent on environmental factors.

**Susceptibilities:** Former Dominant types: see NPA and NA types. Former Passive Aggressive types: see *compliant* and *non-compliant* types.

**Pitfalls:** Unless details of the individuals' lives are known, descriptions of the Resigned types NP−A and N−A can mimic NP and N types, respectively.

### *From Chapter 5: A Model of human behavior*

Resigned types are mature individuals having an aggressive component in their character structure, who have given up the struggle of "playing the game" of dominance and submission, and have entered a state of detachment. We denote the state of suppressed aggression after maturity by −A. We identify two groups of Resigned types: 1) former Dominant types having the trait of aggression, and 2) former non-compliant Passive

Aggressive types. Such individuals carry the mottos: "I am self-sufficient. I am independent of everyone and everything," and "I don't need anyone else, thus no one can hurt me."

Whatever the cause for the detachment, whether it was rooted in genetics, in a single traumatic event such as a disfiguring accident, or in a spectrum of stressful circumstances, the individual has, in essence, taken to the hills. He has felt his psychic equilibrium to be in jeopardy, and in defense he has rationalized a philosophy of resourcefulness and splendid inner independence. He becomes an onlooker of life, or to the extent that he considers himself to be superior to others, he may adopt the attitude of a detached overseer.

## NP−A type

Considering first the NP−A type, he develops a personal philosophy of non-involvement with all things both great and small, perhaps a philosophy of equilibrium or communication with nature. His philosophy may be based on achieving peace through religion or through non-involvement with the environment. As he would consider his involvement with the environment a desecration of the natural order, so does he resent any intrusion of the environment into his life. He will resist acceptance of any philosophy or any way of thinking that may lead to irresolvable problems or to unforeseen conflicts. He may deny the evidence of Darwinian evolution, thereby assuming ultimate independence from the world around him in effectively denying that he is a member of the human race.

He develops his own magic circle of detachment and bitterly resents any unwanted intrusion into it. There is an undercurrent of anxiety with regard to being intruded upon or of being drawn into circumstances that would impose themselves on him. He is constantly scanning the horizon for the approach of events casting their shadows before them, and he is always prepared for escape if the coercion becomes too great. If an escape route is not available, then his anxiety level will rise. He may be literally claustrophobic in constrained situations.

His whole life becomes geared to the maintenance of his detachment. He will seek work in a non-hierarchal structure where the fewest demands are made on him. He will, at all costs, avoid making demands on others. He may become a physician, a taxi driver, a free-lance writer, a nun, a lighthouse keeper or a vagabond. If coerced, he will leave his job abruptly, and the search for another suitable one may take an interminably long time. In sports he is an avid spectator, or if he is active he will row a single scull or be a cross-country jogger.

His personal life is often a mystery to his companions and co-workers. Often no one really knows where he lives or what he does. He may keep an unlisted telephone number and no identifying sign on his door. In a hotel, a "do not disturb" sign appears immediately on his door. He lives and travels alone. And to all observers he appears to live alone and like it.

He is, of course, unaggressive. He is friendly, cordial and good humored. He is reliable, helpful and has a real sense of integrity. He is a person who is well liked by others and is considered to be dependable.

In order to maintain his detachment he must continually be on guard so that friendships do not become overly constraining. Relationships with a sexual connotation become interludes with the understanding that real involvement is not around the corner. The prospect of marriage is frightening unless his prospective mate is able to show the promise of supporting his detached status. His aversion to close friendships and to the expression of giving oneself to another person cannot help but lead to an emotional numbness. He becomes bland and phlegmatic. As he goes through life and is exposed to more and more, he responds by taking less and less. His life has become peaceful, placid with not a conflict in sight, but it has become shallow.

When threatened or goaded, he can be activated to an aggressive state, but like the non-compliant Passive Aggressive type, he is not comfortable there. He will be deeply disappointed with himself that others were able to penetrate his aura of placidity and goad him into "playing the game" once more.

When coerced to the breaking point, he may, once in a lifetime, erupt in a vociferous rage of rebellion, which carries the motto, "To hell with you all! I am not going to do all these things for you anymore! I'm getting out of here!" which will be seen to be a narcissistic rage in disguise.

When not coerced, this NP−A type is a quiet, resourceful worker who has a strong resemblance to the NP Dominant type, "the quiet achiever". However, the Resigned type's residual aggressive component is subtly evident by his occasional aggressive language and gestures. Like all types expressing the aggressive gene, he is prone to the undercurrents of sadistic behavior. In the detached individual this may occur in the form of passive obstructionist behavior reminiscent of the PA type, in the form of non-involvement in situations where disaster is imminent, in the morbid interest in natural disasters such as the following of the progress of a hurricane, or finally in simply standing back in detached amusement and watching the faults and foibles of others as they fritter and flounder about, fumble and fail in their frenetic ventures of futile human folly.

## N −A type

Turning to the N−A Resigned type, according to the model he is lacking in perfectionist qualities. He is less a quiet worker than a narcissistic individual who is well capable of task-oriented accomplishments, but less of directed efforts requiring the planning and execution of many interrelated details. In addition, when activated to the NA+ state, he may resemble the hyperactive, hypersexual "bird of prey" NA type. In such an individual, his only bridge to involvement with others is on a sexual plane, and of course the affairs can lead to no stable relationship.

Finally, as is true for all character types, the Resigned type is vulnerable. If his magic circle comes to be repeatedly penetrated, he may feel the walls of life closing in on him, and he may descend into the profound depression of an abject state.

### From Chapter 6: Character caricatures

The Resigned types NP−A and N−A are much like NPA and NA Dominant types in totally unstressed circumstances. The voice is often somewhat subdued, yet it is usually more forceful, and has greater range, than that of the NP type. The NP−A type preserves the intimate eye contact of his NPA+ cousin. With regard to countenance, the NP−A and N−A types tend toward a sanguine complexion, while the non-sanguine −A and P−A types (schizoid Borderline individuals) tend toward pallor.

The Resigned type often reveals himself not so much by his mannerisms, the tone of his voice or his smile as by the detached life that he leads. In his serenity and in his non-involvement in close relationships he puzzles his colleagues and acquaintances, who may suspect that he has an unconventional sexual orientation. The dynamics of his lifestyle become understandable once his underlying character structure is apparent. These dynamics were presented in Chapter 5 above and will not be repeated here.

Somerset Maugham was obviously fascinated by resigned persons. The protagonist, Larry, of his biographical novel *The Razor's Edge* is a resigned vagabond, and individuals of the Resigned type appear in other of his works as well [22].

# CONCLUSION

## A reminder: they are caricatures

As we mentioned in the Preface, our approach was to present the vignettes of the various NPA types in a caricaturized fashion. It would have been next to impossible to provide descriptions free from pejorative language, so providing *caricatures* allows us to focus on the essential points of the various NPA types, even if their particular characteristics are overblown in the extremes of hyperbolic language.

The reader will have noted that all of the character types had qualities that were, shall we say… somewhat exceptional.

## So, who is normal?

That is actually a very good question. According to the NPA model, no one is really "normal". We all have measures of the three NPA traits, and we have to learn to deal with their implications. It is a natural part of the human condition.

## What are implications of having a particular character type?

How one deals with the realization that one has a particular genetically determined NPA type is a very personal affair. In many respects the constraints of having a particular "genetic" type are similar to the constraints of being male or female. Does being of one sex or the other have its constraints? Of course it does, and we deal with it every day of our lives. Similarly, having a particular NPA type has its limitations, but isn't it better to have a conscious awareness of them, rather than dealing with them unknowingly or unconsciously?

## Where do we go from here?

If the reader is interested in developing a knack for "typing" people according to the NPA model, be they family members, acquaintances or celebrities, we have provided in Appendix C space where one can list names of individuals diagnosed according to NPA category. As one develops these lists, it would be of interest to contemplate the qualities that individuals of a given type have in common, in contrast to qualities that are very variable.

A bibliography is provided for those interested in pursuing our approach further. The works of Karen Horney are still in print, and the reader could not go wrong if he or she started there.

If the reader has an interest in the personality types of historical figures of the past, then an exciting adventure awaits in the biographical section of one's local library. Numerous "pitfalls" await also, but that should make the adventure all the more interesting.

Bon voyage!

# APPENDICES

# APPENDIX A

## NPA PERSONALITY THEORY: SYNOPSIS
### Personality theory based on the genetic traits of sanguinity, perfectionism and aggression

The NPA theory of personality was developed by A.M. Benis on the basis of concepts presented over fifty years ago by psychiatrist Karen Horney. The model posits three major behavioral traits underlying personality: sanguinity (N), perfectionism (P) and aggression (A), leading to the formulation of discrete character types. Each trait is based on a major pleiotropic gene (a gene determining several related characteristics) that follows the rules of Mendelian genetics.

The NPA model proposes that the character traits A and N are indispensable to human development, being related to the sympathetic and parasympathetic nervous systems, respectively. The trait P is also assumed to function at the level of the central nervous system and to act as a modifier of the expression of traits A and N. The NPA model proposes to clarify the genetic bases of known personality disorders, diseases related to behavioral factors ("psychosomatic diseases") and mental illnesses.

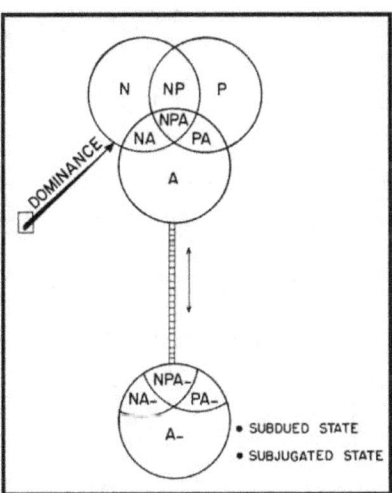

**Fig. A1.** Venn diagram of Dominant character types. Character types having the trait of aggression A may be reduced, reversibly, to a subdued or subjugated state A–.

# **Contents**

# What is personality?

Psychologists speak of personality as "a collection of emotional, thought and behavioral patterns unique to a person that is consistent over time" [1]. Although many investigators have proposed various theories of personality, no objectively testable model has emerged. The NPA model falls into the category of a trait theory of personality, its unique approach being that it is biologically based on classical human genetics.

# NPA model based on three genetic traits

### Genetics and environment

Although it is universally accepted that both genetic and environmental factors (or "nature and nurture") comprise personality, the relevant genes have yet to be identified [2]. Studies of the heritability of personality factors conducted with identical and fraternal twins emphasize the importance of genetics in behavior [3]. The NPA model acknowledges the possible importance of environment and culture in personality but emphasizes that it is the genetic, or structural, factors that first need to be identified.

The NPA model acknowledges that the genetic bases of personality are themselves complex. It assumes at least four tiers to this genetic basis:

- male or female gender

- character type based on the three NPA traits

- temperament, or the degree of activity or excitability of an individual in the Pavlovian sense

- other facets of personality, such as Raymond Cattell's 16 Personality Factors or Hans Eysenck's P-E-N model of personality.

The NPA model, thus, focuses on only the second of these four tiers, acknowledging that temperament and other facets of personality may involve a large number of genes.

**Fig. A2.** Karen Horney (1885-1952)

### Traits of sanguinity, perfectionism and aggression

Karen Horney advanced the concept that at maturity there exist at least three expansive character types, namely the "narcissistic", the "perfectionistic" and the "arrogant-vindictive" [5]. Extending these ideas, the NPA model posits that the human character rests primarily on the existence of three major traits: sanguinity (N), perfectionism (P) and aggression (A). Each of these traits is assumed to exist as the expression of a single major pleiotropic gene. Horney considered that the traits have environmental origins, being the result of an individual's desperate search for dominance in the context of a stifling upbringing [5]. The NPA model — in ascribing the traits to genetic origins — emphasizes biological attributes associated with the traits.

#### Aggression (A)

The behavioral trait of aggression is proposed to be the most labile of the three [6]. The stereotypic acts associated with this trait involve body posturing, gestures, and eye contact of intimidation and deference, with individuals having this trait continually competing with each other on a scale of dominance and submission. The trait of aggression corresponds to a striving for *power* over one's environment, hence it is one main component of competitiveness in social relations, or ambition. In a pejorative connotation the trait may reveal itself in the context of sadism or sadomasochism. The facial expression is non-sanguine, i.e., tending toward sallowness or pallor in individuals of light skin color. The hallmark of the trait of aggression is a mass discharge of the sympathetic nervous system: the "flight or fight" response or the aggressive-vindictive rage. During the expression of this rage, the facial complexion of pallor is accentuated.

### Sanguinity (N)

The trait of sanguinity (Horney's "narcissism") is proposed to be less labile than that of aggression (where individuals may be constantly altering their character states on a scale of dominance and submission) [6]. The stereotypic acts associated with the trait include self-flaunting body posturing, expansive arm gestures, bowing, instinctive self-adornment, and a natural attraction to the limelight of personal recognition. Individuals having only this trait (of the three) are competitive but non-aggressive in their strivings for recognition. The trait corresponds to a striving for *glory* in one's environment, representing the second main component of human ambition. In a pejorative connotation, the unbridled trait of narcissism may reveal itself in the context of conceit, exhibitionism, vanity or messianism. An associated facial expression includes the radiant gingival smile (broadly exposing the gums and teeth). The facial complexion in individuals of light skin color tends toward blood-red or ruddy. Hallmarks of the trait include blushing, flushing, and a mass discharge of the parasympathetic nervous system: the narcissistic rage of defense and withdrawal. During expression of this rage the normally sanguine complexion becomes even more florid.

### Perfectionism (P)

The trait of perfectionism in the NPA model is not a basic drive of ambition and is not associated with a rage reaction [6]. Rather it is a mediator of the unbridled drives of aggression and/or narcissism. The stereotypic acts associated with the trait of perfectionism are obsessiveness, compulsiveness, repetition, and the maintenance of neatness, order and symmetry. A clue to the nature of the trait lies in the compulsive, repetitive mannerisms of autistic children and some adult schizophrenic individuals. The behavioral pattern is often ritualistic and the speech characterized by echolalia. It is posited that such autistic and schizophrenic individuals are those in whom the two components of ambition, i.e., aggression and narcissism, have been suppressed by genetic or environmental factors, either congenitally, in childhood, or after maturity, thus revealing in the individual a primitive state of perfectionism.

# Character types

The notion that humans exhibit only a limited number of discrete character types can be traced back to the time of the ancient Greeks, in particular to the theory of humors (blood, black bile, yellow bile and phlegm). The NPA model attempts to relate genetic NPA types to these character types of antiquity, as well as to the classic personality disorders of modern psychiatry.

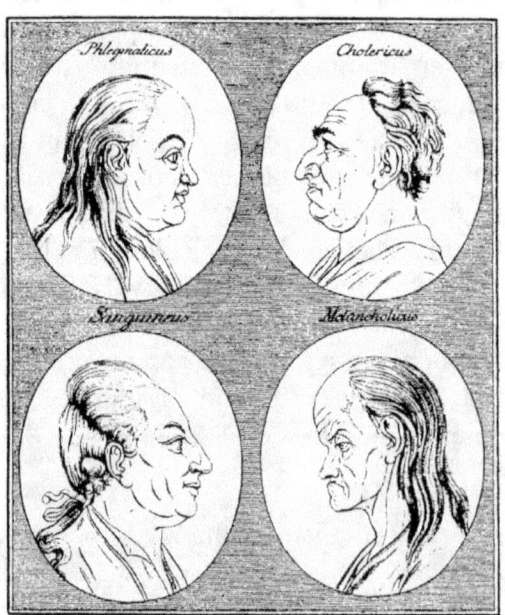

**Fig. A3.** Character types according to the ancient theory of humors: *Phlegmaticus, Cholericus, Sanguineus* and *Melancholicus*. [*J.K. Lavater, ca. 1775*]

## Dominance: Dominant character types

In Dominant types the traits A and N, if present at all, are fully expressed [6]. The NPA model generates the following types:

### N type

The *sanguine (N) type* is found in the writings of Horney [7] and others who have developed the classic psychiatric views of narcissism. In the NPA model this type is the equivalent of the sanguine character type described by the ancients. The important attributes of this type are: expansiveness but unaggressiveness, non-perfectionism, a tendency to flamboyant self-adornment, a natural attraction to the limelight, the gingival smile of recognition and the florid narcissistic rage. In extreme forms this type appears as a self-anointed visionary, a proselytizing evangelist or a messianic personality.

### A type

The *aggressive (A) type* corresponds to Horney's arrogant-vindictive type and to her concept of "moving against people" [8]. In the NPA model this is the classic choleric character type of antiquity. The main attributes of this type are: unbridled arrogance, instinctual vindictiveness, non-perfectionism, no tendency to self-adornment, a wry or sardonic grin in place of a gingival smile, and the pallid-complexioned aggressive-vindictive rage. In extreme forms this type appears as a sadistic personality, as an extroverted paranoid personality, or as the so-called antisocial or sociopathic personality.

### NA type

The *sanguine-aggressive (NA) type* is regarded to be a composite of the previously described sanguine and aggressive types. Horney described the essence of this character type, in the female, in an article, "The overvaluation of love: a study of a common present day type" [9]. The main attributes of this type are: a sanguine complexion, synergistic merging of unbridled narcissism and aggression, hyperactivity, non-perfectionism, a tendency toward extreme self-adornment, exhibitionism in the limelight, a "flashy" extroverted smile and a tendency toward aggressive-vindictive or combined narcissistic-aggressive rages. In extreme forms this type appears as the hypomanic, histrionic or hysterical personality.

## NP type

The attributes of the *sanguine-perfectionistic (NP) type* were described by Horney in her exposition of the "perfectionist type" [4]. In the NPA model this encompasses the classic phlegmatic type known to the ancients. The main qualities of this type are: a tendency toward a sanguine complexion, industriousness, orderliness, an intense sense of duty, unaggressiveness, stubbornness, negativism, a tendency to ruminate, perfectionistic rather than unbridled self-adornment, an uncommonly seen gingival smile of recognition, and the capacity to exhibit the florid narcissistic rage. In extreme forms this character appears as the obsessive-compulsive personality.

## PA type

The *perfectionistic-aggressive (PA) type* is alluded to by Horney in her mention of aggressive types who function in the capacity of a "power behind the throne" [8], that is, personages who utilize intellectual qualities and planning rather than overt aggression to achieve their aims. In the NPA model this is the classic non-sanguine, austere melancholic personality of the ancients. The principal qualities of this type are: a non-sanguine complexion, passive aggressiveness, dour perfectionism, vigilance, manipulativeness, a proud bearing, haughty reservedness, a calculated vindictiveness, a lack of an innate tendency to self-adornment, a sardonic grin, and the pallid-complexioned aggressive-vindictive rage. In extreme forms this is the passive-aggressive, rebellious-distrustful, or ruminating paranoid personality.

## NPA type

The *sanguine-perfectionistic-aggressive (NPA) type* was not explicitly described by Horney, although she did note that the three traits can coexist in the same individual [10]. The main attributes of this type are: a sanguine complexion, a loud voice, dynamism with a tendency to be overbearing, bombastic garrulity, intense eye contact, a strong sense of duty, a bent toward conventional values, unpretentious self-adornment, an outgoing smile of moderate intensity, and the capacity to exhibit the narcissistic, aggressive, or explosive narcissistic-aggressive rages. In the extreme cases this individual is the managerial-autocratic or explosive personality.

## Submission: Passive Aggressive character types

In Passive Aggressive types the trait of aggression is not fully expressed [6]. The NPA model defines two gradations of submission: *non-compliance*, in which the individual is basically submissive but is easily activated to an energetic state of aggression, and *compliance*, in which the individual tends to remain in a profound state of submission.

In the model the state of submission, or inhibition of aggression, most often has a genetic basis, the result of a congenital, inherited, incomplete expression of the gene for the trait A. However, the model also allows for environmental causes, the state of submission being induced during the juvenile period on the basis of environmental constraints to character development. That is, phenocopies (based on environmental factors) of a genetically disposed submissive state may exist. Also, like Dominant types having full expression of the trait A, Passive Aggressive types may exhibit the A rage of aggression.

### Non-compliant types

The model denotes the state of non-compliance by A–, obtaining the following *non-compliant* phenotypes:

- **Aggressive (A–)**
- **Perfectionistic-aggressive (PA–)**
- **Narcissistic (NA–)**
- **Narcissistic-perfectionistic (NPA–)**

### Compliant types

The model denotes the state of compliance by A=, obtaining the following *compliant* phenotypes:

- **Aggressive (A=)**
- **Perfectionistic-aggressive (PA=)**
- **Narcissistic (NA=)**
- **Narcissistic-perfectionistic (NPA=)**

The *NPA– non-compliant type* above corresponds to active, motivated, non-confrontational individuals whose baseline personality tends toward submissiveness, as described by Horney in her discussion of "inverted sadistic" behavior [11]. In the therapeutic setting, these individuals are found over the spectrum of the "Type A", dependent, and phobic-anxious personality. The *NA– type* is a non-perfectionistic, active individual exhibiting pronounced narcissistic behavior. In the therapeutic setting this is a cyclothymic or dependent histrionic personality.

The *compliant types NA=* and *NPA=* above correspond to more profoundly submissive individuals, having more pronounced tendencies toward masochistic behavior [12]. They correspond to Karen Horney's compliant "self-effacing" personality and to her concept of "moving toward people" [13].

## Resignation: Resigned character types

In the character state of resignation the trait of aggression is stunted after maturity because of environmental constraints [6]. Unlike the Passive Aggressive types who readily involve themselves in the relative competition of dominance and submission (and sometimes sadomasochism), Resigned types remain relatively detached from such activities and only with difficulty can be stressed to a state of active aggression. However, like Passive Aggressive types, the Resigned types can be induced into the aggressive-vindictive A rage.

The model denotes the state of resignation by –A, obtaining the following Resigned phenotypes:

- **Aggressive (–A)**
- **Perfectionistic-aggressive (P–A)**
- **Narcissistic (N–A)**
- **Narcissistic-perfectionistic (NP–A)**

The Resigned types having the narcissistic trait correspond to detached individuals, as described by Horney. She considered that "moving away from people" was a maladaptive response that could develop as a growing individual struggled toward maturity [14]. The *NP–A type* would tend to have strong perfectionistic tendencies, while the *N–A type* would be more labile.

## Borderline types and mental illness

In the NPA model *Borderline types* possess only one of the traits of ambition (N or A) and it is only partially expressed. Types in which both traits (N and A) are either absent or profoundly suppressed fall into categories of mental illness, in particular schizophrenia [6]. Thus, NPA theory predicts that the categories of borderline personality and schizophrenia are heterogeneous, depending on the underlying NPA character structure. Examples of Borderline types would be the A– or PA– types above. Types falling into the categories of mental illness would be the compliant Submissive types, A= or PA=.

One aspect of the model focuses on the Dominant types N and NP, which lack the trait A [6]. In analogy with partial expression of the trait A, the theory identifies states of incomplete expression of the trait N, denoted as N–, N= and –N. Examples of Borderline types would be N– or N– P types. Types falling into the categories of mental illness would be N= or N=P, the latter being a perfectionistic, autistic individual.

## Dominance and submission

In the NPA model Dominant character types having the trait A have the potential of being reduced to a subdued state acutely or to a subjugated state chronically (see Fig. A1 above). Similarly, non-compliant Passive Aggressive types have the potential of being activated to an energetic A+ state resembling dominance, usually for short periods of time. Thus, the model emphasizes the potential lability of trait A in social relations, with Dominant and Passive Aggressive types continually altering their behavior in competitive interactions with other individuals and in the context of mating. In the extreme, some of these relationships fall into the category of sadomasochism [15]. Resigned types, in their detachment from social interactions, usually avoid dominance-submission relationships and, in particular, hierarchal structures where "pecking orders" predominate.

## Mendelian transmission of NPA traits

On the basis of archetypal examples, the model assumes that in their full expression the NPA traits are transmitted by autosomal genes, with traits A and N being recessive and trait P being transmitted in the dominant mode [6]. The alleles corresponding to full expression and total suppression of the trait A are denoted by **a** and $A_0$, respectively, and the corresponding alleles for the trait N are denoted by **n** and $N_0$. For the trait P two alleles **P** and $p_0$ are posited, corresponding to full expression or total absence of the trait P, on the assumption that the trait is transmitted with complete penetrance. This scheme of inheritance is consistent with the notion that the alleles $A_0$ and $N_0$ control the production of inhibitors of the traits A and N at the level of the central nervous system, with alleles $A_0$ and $N_0$ being dominant with respect to **a** and **n**. The scheme leads directly to Table A1 below, showing the possible phenotypes of progeny according to the phenotypes of the parents:

The table shows:

- N and A individuals need not have N or A parents. Such individuals can arise *de novo* so long as at least one of the parents is an NP and PA individual, respectively.
- PA individuals must have at least one parent who is of either the PA or A type.
- NP individuals must have at least one parent who is of either the NP or N type.
- NA individuals can arise *de novo* from any combination of phenotypes.
- The mating of two NA types can yield progeny of only NA types.

- The mating of an NPA type with an NA type can yield progeny of only NPA or NA types.

- Certain combinations of parental genotypes may lead to zygotes having only the P trait (P phenotype) or lacking all three traits (null phenotype, denoted by 0). According to NPA theory, zygotes of P or null phenotype would be non-viable. Thus, the model predicts partial or complete infertility in some combinations of parental phenotypes, these being N×A, N×PA, NP×A and NP×PA.

| N | N -- --<br>NA -- --<br>-- -- -- | " | " | " | " | " |
|---|---|---|---|---|---|---|
| A | N -- --<br>NA -- --<br>0 A | -- -- --<br>NA -- --<br>-- A | " | " | " | " |
| NP | N NP --<br>NA NPA --<br>-- -- | N NP P<br>NA NPA PA<br>0 A | N NP --<br>NA NPA --<br>-- -- | " | " | " |
| NA | N -- --<br>NA -- --<br>-- -- | -- -- --<br>NA -- --<br>-- A | N NP --<br>NA NPA --<br>-- -- | -- -- --<br>NA -- --<br>-- -- | " | " |
| PA | N NP P<br>NA NPA PA<br>0 A | -- -- --<br>NA NPA PA<br>-- A | N NP P<br>NA NPA PA<br>0 A | -- -- --<br>NA NPA PA<br>-- A | -- -- --<br>NA NPA PA<br>-- A | " |
| NPA | N NP --<br>NA NPA --<br>-- -- | -- -- --<br>NA NPA PA<br>-- A | N NP --<br>NA NPA --<br>-- -- | -- -- --<br>NA NPA --<br>-- -- | -- -- --<br>NA NPA PA<br>-- A | -- -- --<br>NA NPA --<br>-- -- |
| *FATHER OR MOTHER* | N | A | NP | NA | PA | NPA |

**Table A1.** Possible phenotypes of children according to the phenotypes of the parents. The phenotypes of the father and mother are shown along the axes of the table. The P and null (0) phenotypes by the model are non-viable and would result in miscarriage, stillbirth or an infant who fails to thrive.

# Implications of a trait theory based on genetics

## Population Genetics

A trait theory based on genetics would imply that the personality structure of a population could be expressed in definitive mathematical terms. The NPA model is amenable to the Hardy-Weinberg approach to quantify the distribution of NPA character types in a given subpopulation [16]. With the usual assumptions of gene frequencies $n$, $p$ and $a$ and random mating, incidences of Dominant character types are given in Table A2, below. Because of the occurrence of non-viable P and null (0) phenotypes, the assumptions of Hardy-Weinberg equilibrium would not be strictly valid: the incidences generated by the expressions in Table A2 below represent the phenotypes of the first generation only.

The assumption of numerical values for the three gene frequencies $n$, $p$ and $a$ generates a hypothetical subpopulation, or habitancy [16]. In Table A3 six habitancies are given with descriptive labels: *Polymorphic,* (or "Balanced"), *Punctilious, Sublime, Demonstrative, Authoritarian* and *Militant*. The intent of the labels is to emphasize the very different tenors of each of the distributions of character types.

The table demonstrates that:

- Relatively small changes in gene frequencies could cause large changes in the phenotype frequencies.
- The frequencies of non-viable P and null types are low for these habitancies, on the order of 0 to 8 percent.

Relative incidence of phenotypes on basis of gene frequencies $n$, $p$ and $a$

| Phenotype | Relative incidence |
|---|---|
| N | $n^2 \times (1-p)^2 \times (1-a^2)$ |
| A | $(1-n^2) \times (1-p)^2 \times a^2$ |
| NP | $n^2 \times p(2-p) \times (1-a^2)$ |
| NA | $n^2 \times (1-p)^2 \times a^2$ |
| PA | $(1-n^2) \times p(2-p) \times a^2$ |
| NPA | $n^2 \times p(2-p) \times a^2$ |
| P | $2n(1-n) \times p(2-p) \times 2a(1-a)$ |
| null (0) | $2n(1-n) \times (1-p)^2 \times 2a(1-a)$ |

**Table A2.** Relative incidences of phenotypes for the first generation. The incidence for each phenotype is the product of three probabilities, corresponding to the presence or absence of the three traits N, P and A. The P and null types are non-viable and contribute neither to parentage nor issue.

| | | | HABITANCY | | | |
|---|---|---|---|---|---|---|
| Phenotype | Balanced | Punctilious | Sublime | Demonstrative | Authoritarian | Militant |
| N | 7 | 3 | 77 | 2 | 1 | 1 |
| A | 3 | <1 | <1 | 2 | 17 | 34 |
| NP | 22 | 78 | 18 | 7 | 2 | 1 |
| NA | 13 | <1 | 3 | 20 | 6 | 11 |
| PA | 9 | 2 | <1 | 7 | 52 | 35 |
| NPA | 39 | 8 | 1 | 61 | 17 | 12 |
| P | 4 | 8 | <1 | 1 | 4 | 2 |
| null (0) | 1 | <1 | 1 | <1 | 1 | 2 |
| Gene frequencies | $n = 0.90$ $p = 0.50$ $a = 0.80$ | $n = 0.90$ $p = 0.80$ $a = 0.30$ | $n = 0.99$ $p = 0.10$ $a = 0.20$ | $n = 0.95$ $p = 0.50$ $a = 0.95$ | $n = 0.50$ $p = 0.50$ $a = 0.95$ | $n = 0.50$ $p = 0.30$ $a = 0.95$ |

**Table A3.** Frequencies of phenotypes in six habitancies (per 100 zygotes, or pregnancies). The P and null (0) phenotypes are non-viable. Non-viable types arise when the zygote has neither trait N nor A. The above analysis is confined to Dominant character types on the assumption of two alleles for each NPA gene.

## Evolutionary origins of NPA traits

The assumption of a genetic basis for the traits N, P and A implies that their origins reside in the evolution of humans from precursor species, and in particular, that the traits are likely to be found in primates other than *Homo sapiens*. As examples, the model leads to proposed character types as follows:

- The omnivorous, hierarchal, unsmiling olive baboon, known for its lengthy grooming rituals, would be a likely perfectionist-aggressive PA type.

- The herbivorous, aloof, phlegmatic orangutan and gorilla, capable of gingival smiles, would be likely NP types.

- Akin to humans, the omnivorous, promiscuous chimpanzee, also capable of the gingival smile, would likely have a heterogeneous distribution of types, with NA and NPA types predominating.

**Fig. A4.** NPA theory proposes that the olive baboon is a likely perfectionist-aggressive PA type.

## Predictive aspects of NPA model

The model would have the potential to be predictive in the following categories:

- The possible genetic character types of children could be deduced from the character types of parents.

- Relations could be defined between genetic character type and susceptibility to certain physical and mental diseases.

- Combinations of parental character types prone to infertility problems (miscarriage and stillbirth) could be identified, these combinations being ones which permit the occurrence of a fetus having neither trait N nor A.

- Allele frequencies for the NPA traits, as well as the resultant distributions of NPA character types, in various societies could be analyzed on the basis of well-known principles of population genetics.

- Studies with primates could confirm a biological basis for behavior in the areas of sociobiology and evolutionary psychology.

## Criticism and controversy

Controversy has always followed past positions taken by the scientific community relating human behavior to inheritance, as in Arthur Jensen's theories of intelligence, Herrnstein and Murray's "The Bell Curve", or Lewontin and colleagues' "Not in Our Genes". The NPA personality theory is not exempt. The result of the "nature versus nurture" debate has been that a gauntlet had been thrown to those who espouse genetic underpinnings to behavior: "show us the relevant genes".

The slow progress of unraveling of the genetic basis of personality is the subject of a recent review article by Jang and colleagues [2]. They point out the lack of any genetic framework in the classification of the Diagnostics and Statistical Manual of American psychiatry (DSM-IV), and the pressing need to identify "genetically crisp" characteristics — or genetic traits of behavior that are independent of competing genetic and environmental influences.

The NPA model posits narcissism to be a genetic trait, being related to the parasympathetic branch of the autonomic nervous system, just as aggression is classically related to the sympathetic branch. This concept of narcissism, and the associated narcissistic rage, is not found in any branch of classical medicine or psychiatry and remains a key point requiring validation. Of note is the recent study by Livesley and colleagues [3] with identical and fraternal twins. They found that of a total of eighteen dimensions of personality it was narcissism that had the highest heritability.

The manuscript of the NPA model was copyrighted with the Library of Congress in 1982, being published in book form in 1985 [17] and in a peer-reviewed journal in 1990 [6]. A revised electronic edition in pdf format was released in 2004 and the online NPA personality test in 2005. Studies are in progress utilizing the NPA personality test in obstetric and gynecological patients [18].

Although the NPA model is several decades old, it has not been validated in the sense of withstanding scrutiny by the scientific method — as is true of all other theories of personality as well. Given the recent advances in deciphering the human genome, such scrutiny may soon be possible. The ideas of Karen Horney have been resilient over time, and the validity of her observations that form the basis of the NPA model awaits the relevant studies in the realm of behavioral genetics.

## References

Benis, A.M. *Toward Self and Sanity: On the genetic origins of the human character*, Psychological Dimensions, New York, 1985. ISBN 0884370747 [2nd edition, *The NPA Theory of Personality*, 2008. ISBN 9780615262147]

Benis, A.M. and J.H. Rand (1986). A model of human personality based on Mendelian genetics (abstract).

*Proceedings of the American Association for the Advancement of Science,* Publication 86-5, 124.

Benis, A.M. (1990). A theory of personality traits leads to a genetic model for borderline types and schizophrenia. *Speculations in Science and Technology 13* (3), 167-175.

Freud, Sigmund. "Heredity and the aetiology of the neuroses," in *Early Psycho-analytic Publications,* Hogarth, London, [1896] 1962.

Horney, Karen. *Neurosis and Human Growth*, Norton, 1950.

Horney, Karen. *Our Inner Conflicts*, Norton, 1945.

Horney, Karen. *New Ways in Psychoanalysis*, Norton, 1939.

Horney, Karen. *Feminine Psychology*, Norton, [1922 to 1937] 1967.

Jang, K.L., Vernon, P.A. and W.J. Livesley (2001). Behavioural-genetic perspectives on personality function. *Canadian Journal of Psychiatry 46*, 234-244.

Livesley, W.J., Jang, K.L., Jackson, D.N. and P.A. Vernon (1993). Genetic and environmental contributions to dimensions of personality disorder. *American Journal of Psychiatry 150*, 1826-1831.

Stone, Michael H. *The Borderline Syndromes*, McGraw-Hill, 1980.

## Citations

1. *Personality*, in Wikipedia.

2. Jang *et al.* (2001). Behavioural-genetic perspectives.

3. Livesley *et al.* (1993). Genetic and environmental contributions.

4. Horney, *Neurosis and Human Growth*, Chapter 8: The expansive solutions: the appeal of mastery.

5. Horney, *Neurosis and Human Growth*, Chapter 4: Neurotic pride.

6. Benis (1990). Theory of personality traits leads to genetic model.

7. Horney, *New Ways in Psychoanalysis*, Chapter 5: The concept of narcissism.

8. Horney, *Our Inner Conflicts*, Chapter 4: Moving against people.

9. Horney, *Feminine Psychology*, pp. 182-213.

10. Horney, *New Ways in Psychoanalysis*, p. 97.

11. Horney, *Our Inner Conflicts*, Chapter 12: Sadistic trends.

12. Horney, *New Ways in Psychoanalysis*, Chapter 15: Masochistic phenomena.

13. Horney, *Our Inner Conflicts*, Chapter 3: Moving toward people.

14. Horney, *Our Inner Conflicts*, Chapter 5: Moving away from people.

15. Horney, *Neurosis and Human Growth*, Chapter 10: Morbid dependency.

16. Benis, *Toward Self and Sanity*, Chapter 10: Genetics.

17. Benis, *Toward Self and Sanity*.

18. by Donna K. Hobgood, M.D., Clinical Attending Physician, University of Tennessee College of Medicine, Chattanooga.

## Illustrations

Karen Horney: "Studio photo" courtesy of Karen Horney Papers, Manuscripts and Archives, Yale University Library, New Haven. Copyright unknown.

Character types according to theory of humors: From Johann Kaspar Lavater, *Physiognomics*, ca. 1775.

Olive baboon: U.S. Fish and Wildlife Service.

## Source

This article originally appeared in *Wikipedia*, the online encyclopedia in May 2006. It was later deleted for reasons of non-notability. The reference was: "NPA personality theory", *Wikipedia, The Free Encyclopedia,* 2 July 2006, Wikimedia Foundation:
http://en.wikipedia.org/wiki/NPA_personality_theory.

# APPENDIX B
# The Morbid Dependency

The term "morbid dependency" was introduced by Karen Horney (see *Neurosis and Human Growth*, 1950). In the NPA model the morbid dependency appears as an extreme in dominance-submissive relationships, limited to types that have a component of the A trait in their character structure. Thus, N and NP types do not participate in the dynamics that are portrayed here.

The excerpt below is from our book: Chapter 9: *Interactions between character types* [23]. Following Karen Horney, we use mainly masculine pronouns, although the accounts apply equally to male and female individuals.

## The morbid dependency

In a "morbid dependency" individuals who have an aggressive component in their character structure have the innate drive to "play the game" of dominance and submission. When two such individuals enter a long-term relationship, one of them establishes dominance over the other. This is the chronic state of subjugation of which we have spoken, and if both partners accept the status of the relationship, it may appear to be a stable one. However, as we have pointed out, the relationship is essentially one of master ruling over slave, and in this context there is always the risk of sadomasochistic elements entering into the relationship. In addition, the master being the omnipotent master that he is, he will feel himself to be well within his rights to terminate the relationship at any time.

The nature of the relationship that ensues in the chronic state of subjugation depends, to a large extent, on the nature and intensity of the sadistic trends in the dominant individual. These were discussed in some detail in the previous chapter [24], and were seen to lie in the realm of the individual's basic character structure, as well as in other intrinsic and extrinsic forces in life that tend to suppress overt sadistic behavior.

One could describe an infinite number of relationships based on the chronic state of subjugation, each with its particular nuances. On the one hand, we find the most overt sadomasochistic relationship based on outright cruelty and violence. At the other end of the spectrum, we find the self-condemned couple whose life together is a morass of overt and inverted sadomasochistic behavior. This is the silent couple that we see in the restaurant. The master is gloomy, and his eyes are averted from his companion, the slave. The latter is unhappy and looks intermittently to his mate in a deferential manner for recognition. And recognition, when it comes, is only grudgingly pronounced. These two individuals know that something is wrong, but they have only the foggiest notion of what it is.

This subtle state of affairs may involve even the usually dutiful NPA+ type in either the dominant or submissive role. As a dominant subjugator, the NPA type's sense of duty causes his sadistic trends to be deeply inverted, and if they do break out into overtness, he periodically hates himself for it. In the subjugated role, the NPA type suffers. He suffers because of the dramatic personality split he must assume when in the presence of his master. Furthermore, he is periodically driven to the extremes of frustration, which cannot help but incite him to his NPA super-rages. And in the wake of these rages he senses only a continuation of his confused frustration, and a growing suspicion that just as he is not in control of his emotions, he is equally not in control of his life situation.

A chronic state of subjugation between two individuals can exist, in a seemingly stable relationship, for many years. However, the illusory nature of this stability is revealed time and time again, as we can readily confirm in the real life situations that intersect our lives. Sometimes the relationship, in all of its apparent placidity, may take on the appearances of a nice, tranquil, uneventful voyage... of the Hindenburg on its last transatlantic crossing.

If the relationship is a fairly stable one, we think that it is appropriate to call it a dependency of subjugation. If the relationship is an unstable one, with more pronounced sadomasochistic trends, and the dependent partner is at risk of destroying himself or murdering his mate, then we think that Karen Horney's term "morbid dependency" is appropriate.

The essential dynamics of the morbid dependency have been noted throughout the ages. The American psychologist William James called it "monomania" and presented dramatic examples of in his treatises published at the turn of the 19th century [25]. Somerset Maugham and Karen Horney were both intrigued by the dynamics of the morbid dependency, in part because of their own life experiences. One can hardly improve on their perspicacious expositions of the subject, and the reader is referred to Maugham's *Of Human Bondage* and Horney's *Neurosis and Human Growth*.

Maugham, at least in his early years, apparently viewed the morbid dependency as the basis of all love relationships. In the words of Philip in *Of Human Bondage*:

"I'm afraid that's always the case," he said. "There's always one who loves and one who lets himself be loved."

In our view, the morbid dependency is a fundamental type of behavior limited to personages having an aggressive component in their character structures, i.e., the A, NA, PA or NPA Dominant types and the Passive Aggressive types.

The basic forces involved in the morbid dependency are straightforward. It is the role of the master to rule over his slave, using all of the dynamics of sadomasochistic behavior that are available to him. It is the role of the slave to accept all that is meted out to him, so long as the master does not leave him.

Following Horney [26], the compendium of actions available to the master is:

- to enslave
- to punish
- to frustrate
- to exploit
- to play on emotions
- to use vindictive violence, and
- to show complete lack of feelings toward his companion.

The dynamics of the morbid dependency are not limited to love relationships. They may enter wherever there is evidence of dominant-submissive behavior. This may occur in the context of leader and follower, boss and subordinate, priest and penitent, parent and child, physician and patient, or guard and prisoner. It may, of course, appear in a sexual setting, and the overt rituals of sexual sadomasochistic behavior are a well-known fact of life. It should be clear, however, that there is nothing intrinsically sexual about the sadomasochistic relationship of the morbid dependency. If the two partners are of the same sex, homosexuality is not necessarily implied.

We shall describe an extreme, full-blown case in which the two partners embrace upon a path leading to destruction, or at least to a lack of fulfillment. The master and slave can be of any of the NPA types that have a measure of the A trait, although Passive Aggressive types will most often play the role of the dependent partner. It goes without saying that neither partner understands the other, neither understands the nature of the relationship, and neither understands himself.

Soon after the initial excitement of a new relationship, in all of its sexual and non-sexual aspects, the master-slave relationship begins to emerge. Even at this early stage, small, barely noticeable horns will begin to grow from the forehead of the master. The slave, though, is hooked: he is devoted to true love until the ends of time.

At a fairly early stage, the master senses his power over the slave. The slave is "in his clutches". He has him "on a string". His partner will "do anything for me". This will be rationalized in the sense that the master enjoys "having things done" for him, or enjoys the constant attention that he receives in a sexual context. But as the initial excitement passes and the subjugation becomes more marked, the inevitable scenario unfolds. The master begins to avert his eyes from the slave, and his initial feelings of attraction turn into gloomy numbness. The master begins to ignore the slave, and the elements of overt, inverted or situational sadism come to the fore. The relationship begins to sour. The illogic of it in its real life setting may be stupefying. The master may consciously or unconsciously, overtly or covertly, begin to search for a new partner. He may make, in similar ways, intimations that the slave simply is not included in his future plans. In everything that the master says or does, there is a subliminal voice saying, "I am going to leave you… I am going to leave you… I am going to leave you…"

Despite all of the illogic in the relationship, even when he sees himself abused, the slave does not give up. On the contrary, he becomes more persistent, more clinging, more groveling, and at the same time more demanding.

It is at this point that the slave begins to feel himself being torn apart in conflict. On the one hand are his feelings of unlimited devotion to his partner, the desire to be taken in his arms to be merged with him, to disappear into him, so that they may at last be one and the same. On the other hand is the feeling of being abused, of giving everything and receiving nothing. And, in flashes, the subjugated partner sees in himself the first inklings of vindictiveness.

As the relationship deteriorates and the master's intimations of leaving become more apparent, the slave may strike out in an attempt to achieve a full-blown submissive triumph [27]. He implores that he has been so devoted, so faithful, so loving, hence he demands to be loved unconditionally in return. The master loved him before, did he not, hence he must love him forever. And as he clings more and more, and grovels before the master, the latter cannot but shrink away. And as the slave promises in an ever-intensifying manner, warmth, favors, gifts and fidelity, the master cannot but grow colder.

If the attempts at a submissive triumph do not succeed, then the slave may descend into an abject state of suffering, for example in a basement or in a darkened room. The state of suffering is in part a further call to be rescued, by anyone, from being left alone in the cruel world. It is partly vindictive, to shame the master before his children, his friends and his neighbors: "See how rotten I am being treated!" And in fact, the dependent partner breaks out of the abject state periodically in vindictive rages of frightening intensity, frightening to everyone including the individual himself. But in the threats of vindictiveness and in the brief skirmishes of violence, the slave realizes that it is all for naught. For after each spell of vindictiveness, he is filled with remorse. And behind the remorse lies the paralyzing fear that his vindictiveness might be the last straw to cause the master to leave.

But for the master to leave? Impossible! Somehow the words have no meaning and do not enter into the reality of the slave. It is just not possible, to the thinking of the slave that this couple who once loved together could ever part.

At this point, the slave may surface from the abject state of suffering, perhaps with the help of a friend, a physician, or a psychiatrist. He will go alone, to some secluded spot, taking a pen and pads of yellow lined paper with him. He will try to figure this out. He is convinced that he will be able to decide in the calm of solitude — either yes or no — whether or not he loves the master. In fact, does he *love* him or does he *hate* him? The question is rarely answered in any definitive terms, but what does emerge on paper is a master plan. The plan is to "turn the tables" on the master, with vindictive elements showing themselves unabashedly. The plan is: "If he does this, then I shall do that." "If he says this, I shall say that." "I shall force him to make the moves." "I just don't care about him anymore, so if he wants something, he will have to ask me." And so on.

However, when the time comes to put the plan into effect, all of the careful planning and all of the self-exhortation is for naught! At the first word from the master, all the plans collapse like a house of cards. The slave is shocked to realize that despite all of his planning, all of his logical thinking, the situation is not amenable to logic at all! The master remains the master, and he remains an utterly powerless slave.

As a relationship of morbid dependency nears its end, two somewhat opposing forces come increasingly into play:

On the one hand, in the dependent partner, there is an ever-increasing anxiety of the ambiguity of the situation, and the situation is, indeed, always ambiguous in the eyes of the slave. For no matter how dismal the outlook is for the success of the relationship, the slave will always have a small hope that, somehow, the master will change his mind, and everything will turn out all right. Or vindictive daydreaming may be prominent: "Just you wait Henry Higgins! When you smash yourself to pieces, you'll come to me as a quadriplegic begging me to take care of you for the rest of your life." And, it is true, the master will sense that all of this ambiguity is to his advantage. He has, practically, no need to do anything. Until he decides what is to be done, for the good of all concerned, he can profit from the ambiguity of the situation to play on the emotions of the slave.

On the other hand, there is an ever-increasing weariness, a gradually intensifying numbness on the part of the dependent partner. He begins to look forward to the end of the relationship. He thirsts for that intense pleasure, in suffering, of knowing that he is right in being wronged. He will find great satisfaction in being physically maltreated at the end of a relationship. He may have dreams of destroying himself at the doorstep of his offending master in a final act of masochistic martyrdom.

After the master leaves, he often comes back. In one way or another he returns to the slave. And the master himself may not really understand why he does so. First of all, he may return in a subdued or even abject state. He may have realized that it is a cold, cruel world out there, and in his inability to cope with it all and in his inability to establish lasting relationships with others, he wonders why he was unable to respond to the tender devotion of the slave. Secondly, he may observe with burning envy that the slave is doing quite well without him. In fact, he cannot bear to see any independence, resourcefulness or levity in any of his subjugated subjects. In consequence, the master may periodically visit his slaves in order to prove to them, and to himself, that he is the lord and master of all the underlings in his life. Finally, if his sadistic trends are marked, he will derive enjoyment and exhilaration from showing up from time to time in order to play on the emotions of his slaves. The latter, despite all logic, remain helplessly subjugated by the master [28].

# APPENDIX C
## Personal log of NPA types

*Dominant*

### N                                          A

_____          _____

_____          _____

_____          _____

_____          _____

_____          _____

_____          _____

_____          _____

_____          _____

_____          _____

_____          _____

_____          _____

_____          _____

_____          _____

_____          _____

_____          _____

_____          _____

_____          _____

## *Dominant*

| NA | NP |
|----|----|
| _____ | _____ |
| _____ | _____ |
| _____ | _____ |
| _____ | _____ |
| _____ | _____ |
| _____ | _____ |
| _____ | _____ |
| _____ | _____ |
| _____ | _____ |
| _____ | _____ |
| _____ | _____ |
| _____ | _____ |
| _____ | _____ |
| _____ | _____ |
| _____ | _____ |
| _____ | _____ |
| _____ | _____ |
| _____ | _____ |
| _____ | _____ |
| _____ | _____ |
| _____ | _____ |
| _____ | _____ |

*Dominant*

| PA | NPA |
|----|-----|
|    |     |
|    |     |
|    |     |
|    |     |
|    |     |
|    |     |
|    |     |
|    |     |
|    |     |
|    |     |
|    |     |
|    |     |
|    |     |
|    |     |
|    |     |
|    |     |
|    |     |
|    |     |
|    |     |

## Passive Aggressive, with P trait

### NPA−

### NPA=

| Passive Aggressive, non-P<br>NA– & NA= | Resigned<br>NP–A & N–A |
|---|---|
| _____ | _____ |
| _____ | _____ |
| _____ | _____ |
| _____ | _____ |
| _____ | _____ |
| _____ | _____ |
| _____ | _____ |
| _____ | _____ |
| _____ | _____ |
| _____ | _____ |
| _____ | _____ |
| _____ | _____ |
| _____ | _____ |
| _____ | _____ |
| _____ | _____ |
| _____ | _____ |
| _____ | _____ |
| _____ | _____ |
| _____ | _____ |
| _____ | _____ |
| _____ | _____ |

# GLOSSARY

**aggressive rage (A rage)** Mass discharge of the sympathetic nervous system related to the A trait of aggression.

**autism** Developmental disorders characterized by difficulty in social communication, in forming relationships with other people and in using language and abstract concepts.

**autonomic nervous system** The portion of the nervous system governing many activities that are not under conscious control. It is composed of two parts: the *sympathetic* and *parasympathetic* nervous systems.

**bipolar disorder** A major disorder of the emotional tone of the individual. It is characterized by severe mood swings toward mania, depression or both.

**blushing** A response of flushing in an emotional context, in the skin of the face, neck and upper chest. According to the model, individuals having the N trait have an increased predisposition to blushing and flushing.

**Borderline type** An NPA type where neither trait N nor A is fully expressed.

**breed true** In genetics, a trait is said to breed true if two parents of the same phenotype always produce offspring of that same phenotype exclusively. In the model, the NA type is the only one that always breeds true: any two NA types will always have only NA offspring.

**cognition** The acts of thinking, feeling, knowing, reasoning and learning, including both awareness and judgment.

**Compliant type** A Passive Aggressive character type having profound inhibition of the A trait (denoted by A=).

**dominant trait**     Refers to Mendelian dominance. Not to be confused with *Dominant type*.

**Dominant type**     An NPA type in which the traits N and/or A are fully expressed. The six types are: N, A, NA, NP, PA, NPA.

**energetic state**     An individual having the A− trait can assume a transient energetic state resembling dominance (A+) by undergoing a *personality split*.

**exhibitionism**     Tendency toward display or extravagant behavior. Exhibitionism is most often a manifestation of the *unbridled* N trait.

**explosive personality**     Characterized by volcanic outbursts of rage, or of verbal or physical aggressiveness.

**extrovert**     An individual whose attention and interests are directed primarily toward others.

**"fight-or-fight" reaction**     Behavioral response associated with mass discharge of the *sympathetic nervous system*, as described by the American physiologist W.B. Cannon.

*folie à deux*     A condition in which two persons, usually closely related, share similar paranoid delusions.

**gene**     A fundamental unit of heredity, composed mainly of DNA. Genes are arranged in linear order on the chromosomes.

**gingival smile**     A broad smile, revealing the gums of the upper teeth, related to the N trait.

**Horney, Karen (1885–1952)**     German-American psychiatrist of Dutch and Norwegian heritage.

**hypomanic**     In psychiatric terms, an individual who has a heightened emotional tone. In *mania* the individual is psychotic and usually requires hospitalization.

**habitancy**    In NPA population genetics, the inhabitants of a region, taken collectively, or a subpopulation. For ease of communication we define the following habitancies:

*Polymorphic* — a mixture of NPA character types
*Sublime* — mainly N types (sanguine)
*Punctilious* — ... NP types (sanguine)
*Corybantic* — ... NA types (sanguine)
*Demonstrative* — ... NPA types (sanguine)
*Authoritarian* — ... PA types (non-sanguine)
*Militant* — ... A types (non-sanguine)
*Introspective* — ... NPA– types (sanguine)

**introvert**    An individual whose interests are predominantly concerned with his own mental life.

**Maugham, W. Somerset (1874-1965)**    English novelist, playwright and world traveler.

**morbid dependency**    A symbiotic relationship based on the trait of aggression, essentially sadomasochistic in nature, between individuals assuming dominant and submissive roles.

**narcissism**    From Narcissus, the figure in Greek mythology who fell in love with his own reflected image. In the present model, narcissism is related to the genetic N trait of sanguinity.

**narcissistic arms gesture**    A gesture of recognition in which the arms are extended to the front or sides, with the fingers slightly spread apart.

**narcissistic personality disorder (NPD)**    In the NPA model patients diagnosed with NPD will likely be individuals having the *unbridled* N trait, mostly NA and N types.

**narcissistic rage (N rage)**    Mass discharge of the autonomic nervous system related to the N trait of sanguinity.

**Non-compliant type**    A Passive Aggressive character type having partial inhibition of the A trait (denoted by A–).

**non-sanguine**    Refers to individuals who lack the trait N.

**paranoia**   A behavioral pattern characterized by hypersensitivity, suspicion, jealousy, envy and a tendency to blame others and ascribe evil motives to them.

**"passive-aggressive"**   A behavioral pattern characterized by obstructionism, procrastination and intentional inefficiency.

**Passive Aggressive type**   An NPA type where trait A is partially inhibited by genetics or environment.

**perfectionism**   The P trait of the model, often appearing in behavior as the achievement of order by persistence and repetition.

**personality**   A collection of behavioral patterns unique to an individual that is consistent over time.

**personality split**   According to the model, individuals having the A or A− trait may transiently assume the converse subdued (A−) and energetic (A+) states, respectively.

**phenotype**   The observable traits in an individual. The NPA character types (N, NP, NA, etc.) are phenotypes.

**"playing the game"**   Individuals having a measure of the trait of aggression constantly "play the game" of dominance and submission.

**pleiotropism**   The determination of multiple characteristics by a single gene.

**power behind throne**   A symbiotic relationship between a PA individual (the Power) and a figurehead individual on whom he depends.

**psychosis**   A major mental disorder in which the individual's ability to interpret reality is grossly impaired.

**resignation**   The state in which an aggressive individual at maturity renounces the "playing of the game" of dominance and submission and adopts a philosophy of independence.

**Resigned type**   An NPA type in which trait A is inhibited by environmental factors after maturity in an individual who was formerly either 1) a Dominant A, PA, NA or NPA type, or 2) a Passive Aggressive type.

**sadism**    Satisfaction derived from aggressively dominating or abusing others.

**sadomasochism**    A symbiotic relationship between two individuals based on the trait of aggression.

**sanguine, sanguinity**    According to ancient physiology, belonging to one of the four "temperaments" in which blood predominates over the other three "humors", leading to a ruddy countenance and exuberant behavior. In the NPA model a sanguine character type is any type having the N trait.

**schizoid**    Withdrawn; tending to avoid close relationships with others.

**smile**    According to the model, the social smile of recognition is based on the N trait of sanguinity.

**subdued state**    An individual having fully expressed trait A can be reduced to a transient subdued state resembling submission (A–) by undergoing a *personality split*.

**subjugated state**    A chronic state resembling submission of an individual with respect to his companion or mate.

**Submissive type**    A *compliant* Passive Aggressive character type who adopts a life style of submissiveness.

**symbiosis**    A relationship between two individuals that has elements of mutual advantage.

**sympathetic nervous system**    A division of the autonomic nervous system that controls, among other functions, the "fight-or flight" response related to the trait of aggression.

**temperament**    The general level of activity, reactivity or excitability of an individual in the Pavlovian sense. An individual of a particular NPA type can be of high or low temperament.

**unbridled trait**    The presence of fully expressed trait N or A without modulation by the P trait.

# REFERENCES & NOTES

**Introduction**

[*1*] Benis (1985, 2008). See also Appendix A.

[*2*] Benis (1985, 2008). See also Appendix A. The gingival smile is also seen in various other Primates, including Old World monkeys and the great apes.

**Chapter 1: N type**

[*3*] Benis (1985, 2008). Chapter 5: *A Model of Human Behavio*r and Chapter 6: *Character Caricatures.*

[*4*] Aristotle on narcissistic behavior, from Loomis (1943): "Conceited people, on the other hand, are fools ignorant of themselves, who make themselves conspicuous by being so; they try for positions of honor under an impression of their own abilities, and then, if they get them, prove failures. They rig themselves up in fine clothes and pose for effect, and so on; they wish what good fortune they have to be known to the world, and talk about themselves, as if that were the road to honor... So boastful people, if their object is reputation, pretend to the qualities that win praise or congratulation, and, if their object is gain, pretend to qualities useful to their neighbors, their own lack of which cannot easily be proved, as, for example, a skill in prophesying or in healing..."

[*5*] Castelot (1965). The author's description of Josephine is practically a caricature: "... It is true and it had often embarrassed him that Josephine, with a Creole's naive and unthinking immorality, often talked shamelessly of her former lovers... She seldom, if ever, read anything and holding a pen tired her out. Only the pleasure of adorning herself, ordering a dress, matching a ribbon for her hair could arouse her from indolence... She was said to have no brains. But she appeared to have enough, or at least to be very clever at making the most of what she had. Her rival, Mme de Vaudey, said she had 'only a quarter of an hour's wit a day'..."

**Chapter 2: A type**

[*6*] Benis (1985, 2008). Chapter 8: *Love & Evil.*

**Chapter 3: NA type**

[*7*] Benis (1985, 2008). Chapter 8: *Love & Evil.* See Appendix B.

[*8*] Le Gallienne (1955).

[*9*] The letter reveals aspects of both dominance and vulnerability. From Gannett newspapers, *The Daily Item,* August 12, 1980: "Dear Ann Landers: I'm a 26-year-old career woman, and lately I've been experiencing severe anxiety attacks — shortness of breath, pounding heart, sweaty palms, feelings of weakness and dizziness. Sometimes my hands shake so I can't hold anything... I can't understand what is causing these symptoms. I'm doing well in my career and enjoy my work. My social life isn't great, but this doesn't bother me. I'd rather stay home than go with some of the creeps I see around town. Can you help me find some answers? — Wassau, Wis."

[*10*] In this short story, Maugham captures a vivid image of the lability of an NA type. From *Rain* (1951): "... They saw Miss Thompson standing at the threshold. But the change in her appearance was extraordinary. This was no longer the flaunting hussy who had jeered at them in the road, but a broken, frightened woman... She stood at the door with the tears streaming down her face... [*Later, after she achieves a vindictive triumph*...] Miss Thompson was standing at her door, chatting with a sailor. A sudden change had taken place in her... She was dressed in all her finery... with the high shiny boots over which her fat legs bulged in their cotton stockings; her hair was elaborately arranged; and she wore that enormous hat covered with gaudy flowers. Her face was painted, her eyebrows were boldly black, and her lips were scarlet. She held herself erect. She was the flaunting queen that they had known at first. As they came in she broke into a loud, jeering laugh..."

### Chapter 4: NP type

[*11*] As an example of an NP type, we presented the following account of Dieter's father, the parent of an autistic child (Bosch, 1970). "Dieter's father had worked his way up via elementary school and a trade apprenticeship in evening classes to the position of civil engineering technician and got his engineer's diploma at the late age of forty-six. He was a do-it-yourself addict and was engrossed in technology. Outside his job he was reportedly somewhat out of touch with the rest of the world. He had a habit of composing long, typewritten reports about his son with dates carefully set out in the margins and many underlinings of points that he thought important... While Dieter was with us at the hospital and he was away on holiday, he wrote his son a letter which, apart from the first sentence dealing with the nice place the parents were staying at, was exclusively given over to a description of all the locomotives complete with type number and colour that the couple had seen during their journey to the resort."

[*12*] e.g., Catherine of Aragon or Tsar Nicholas II.

[*13*] Herndon's biography (1888) is of special interest, as it is a contemporary account that focuses on the personal characteristics of Lincoln: "... His penmanship, after some practice, became so regular in form that it excited the admiration of other and younger boys... He was a very sensitive man modest to the point of diffidence and often hid himself in the masses to prevent the discovery of his identity. He was not indifferent, however, to approbation and public opinion. He had no disgusting egotism and no pompous pride, no aristocracy, no haughtiness, no vanity. Merging together the qualities of his nature he was a meek, quiet, unobtrusive gentleman... He was unusually considerate of the feelings of other men, regardless of their rank, condition, or station. At first sight he struck one with his plainness, simplicity of manner, sincerity, candor, and truthfulness... Lincoln's melancholy never failed to impress any man who ever saw or knew him. The perpetual look of sadness was his most prominent feature..."

[*14*] Benis (1985, 2008). Chapter 11: *Disorders of Human Behavior.*

[*15*] The lack of innate aggression is a striking feature of many children diagnosed with autism. Bosch (1980) gives an account by a German boy, Richard: "... 'Resteten' was the name I gave to my dream world, a world full of harmony and peace in which nothing evil happened, a world rotating round some distant sun far out in the universe. When I was a small boy, whenever life here on earth seemed difficult and incomprehensible, I liked to retire there to its majestic mountain scenery through which the fast-running Olympia River flowed. This happened very often. For from my earliest childhood on I was different from the others of my age, and for children this is of course sufficient reason to mock, punch, and torture. I was unable to defend myself, because a deep-rooted feeling prevented me from raising my hand to hurt another. As a result mixing with schoolmates, which is for most people an enjoyable part of going to school, was torture for me..."

**Chapter 5: PA type**

[*16*] Benis (1985, 2008). Chapter 8: *Love & Evil.*

[*17*] As usual, Maugham focuses on small details that bring the character to life: "... He was now twenty-three and he was still the lanky fellow, though only of average height, that he had always been... He was shabbily dressed in a brown jacket and gray flannel trousers and wore neither hat nor great coat. His long face was thinner and paler than ever and his black eyes seemed larger. They were never still. Hard, shining, inquisitive, suspicious, they seemed to indicate the quality of the brain behind. His mouth was large and ironical, and he had small

irregular teeth that somewhat reminded you of one of the smaller beasts of prey. With his pointed chin and prominent cheek-bones he was not good-looking, but his expression was so high-strung, there was in it so strange a disquiet, that you could hardly have passed him in the street without taking notice of him. At fleeting moments his face had a sort of tortured beauty, not a beauty of feature but the beauty of a restless, striving spirit... A disturbing thing about him was that there was no gaiety in his smile, it was a sardonic grimace, and when he laughed his face was contorted as though he were suffering from an agony of pain. His voice was high-pitched; it did not seem to be quite under his control, and when he grew excited often rose to shrillness..."

## Chapter 6: NPA type

[*18*] Aristotle, in Loomis (1943).

[*19*] In our book, we include an account of an American baseball game, in which the A and N components of a rage can be seen (*The Daily Item*, September 3, 1980): "NEW YORK — In case you missed it, Lou Piniella went 2-for-4 Tuesday night at Yankee Stadium as the Yanks handed the Oakland A's their sixth straight loss, 6 to1... Problem is, Piniella thought he should have been 3-for-4. In the bottom of the seventh, he hit a liner to right, and Tony Armas, after a long run, dropped the ball... 'Error, right fielder,' said official scorer Harold Rosenthal, a retired member of the Baseball Writers' Association of America and well-known author... At second base, Piniella spread his arms wide apart, in total disbelief... That was half the fun. After the game, it was vintage Piniella, howling, screaming and storming. 'I'm going to strangle him,' Piniella roared. 'I'm going to his house and choke him... If they don't change that scoring and give me a hit,' Piniella continued, 'I'm through playing baseball for the year. I quit this game'..."

## Chapter 7: NPA= type

[*20*] In our book we included an account taken from a letter to a newspaper columnist (*The New York Post*, Sept 10, 1980): "Dear Dr. Brothers: Whoever said life begins at 40 was a terrible liar. For me, it seems to be the end of the line. Everything has happened wrong for me in the past two years. ... I had a husband who took care of everything for me, and then he suddenly died. He took care of all the family business; he never even allowed me to drive an automobile because he preferred to do it for me... I'm ashamed to say I don't know how to balance a checkbook or do any of the things that seem to be a part of daily living for a lot of people. I'd like to find another man just like my husband, but

now I'm 42, and it seems unlikely that such a man could ever come along. I'm very depressed most of the time, and I feel that my life is over."

### Chapter 8: NPA− type

[*21*] As an example of a non-compliant type attracted to writing, we give the following account excerpted from a newspaper column ("Hers", L. S. Schwartz, *New York Times*, October 10, 1980): "… His first paper was a shocker. I was surprised to receive it at all — I had him pegged as the sullen type who would give up at the first difficult assignment, then complain that college was irrelevant. On the contrary, the paper, formidably intelligent, jarred my view of the fitness of things. It didn't seem possible — no, it didn't seem right — that a person so sullen and mute should be so eloquent… I do know that I had never before sat transfixed in disbelief over a student paper… The next day I called him over after class and asked if he was aware that he had an extraordinary mind. He said, yes, he was. Close up, there was nothing arrogant about him. A bit awkward and shy, yet gracious, with something antique and courtly in his manner. Why did he never speak in class, I asked… He didn't like to speak in front of people. His voice and his eye turned evasive, like an adolescent's, as he told me this. Couldn't in fact. Couldn't speak… What do you mean, I said. You're not a kid. You have a lot to say. You write like this and you sit in class like a statue? What's it all about? …"

### Chapter 10: NP −A & N −A types

[*22*] The following excerpt from *The Narrow Corner* describes the character Dr. Saunders: "… He was very easy to get on with. He was much liked. But he had no friends. He was an agreeable companion, but neither sought intimacy nor gave it. There was no one in the world to whom he was not at heart indifferent. He was self-sufficient. His happiness depended not on persons but on himself. He was selfish, but since he was at the same time shrewd and disinterested, few knew it and none was inconvenienced by it. Because he wanted nothing, he was never in anybody's way. Money meant little to him, and he never much minded whether patients paid him or not … He had great natural kindliness, but it was a kindliness of instinct, which betokened no interest in the recipient: he would come to the rescue if you were in a fix, but if there was no getting you out of it would not bother about you further. He did not like to kill living things, and he would neither shoot nor fish… Perhaps he was an intensely logical man… but if motive counts for righteousness, then he deserved no praise; for he was influenced in his actions neither by love, pity, nor charity…"→

A several-page essay on Resigned types is buried in *The Gentleman in the Parlour*, an account of Maugham's travels in the Far East: "...We are gregarious, most of us, and we resent the man who does not seek the society of his fellows...But there are people who do not feel at home in the world... They are self-sufficient, and they shrug a resigned and sometimes, it must be admitted, a scornful shoulder because the world uses that adjective in a depreciatory sense. Wherever they are they feel themselves 'out of it'...They may not be very useful members of society, but their lives are harmless and innocent. If the world despises them, they on their side despise the world. The thought of returning to its turmoil is a nightmare to them. They ask nothing but to be left in peace. Their satisfaction with their lot is sometimes a trifle irritating. It needs a good deal of philosophy not to be mortified by the thought of persons who have voluntarily abandoned everything that for the most of us makes life worth living and are devoid of envy of what they have missed. I have never made up my mind whether they are fools or wise men. They have given up everything for a dream, a dream of peace or happiness or freedom, and their dream is so intense that they make it true."

### Appendix B: The morbid dependency

[*23*] Benis (1985, 2008). Chapter 9: *Interactions Between Character Types*. In this chapter we considered two types of symbiotic relationships: the "power behind the throne" and the "morbid dependency".

[*24*] Benis (1985, 2008). Chapter 8: *Love & Evil.*

[*25*] James (1890, 1908).

[*26*] Horney (1945). Chap. 12: *Sadistic Trends.*

[*27*] See "triumphs", in Benis (1985, 2008). Chapter 7: *Justification of One's Existence.*

[*28*] In our book, we included this letter to a newspaper columnist (*New York Post,* August 14, 1980): "Dear Meg: I've been in love with a man I'll call George for three years. For various reasons we broke up I was pulling myself together and getting ready to start all over again when George called. He didn't want to come back, he just wanted to talk. So we talked. The following week he called again. Now he calls just often enough to keep my emotions in complete turmoil. This man cheated on me with other women and broke his word when we entered a business deal. Now he's accusing me of giving him the bum's rush. I admit I still care for him but I know I should put him out of my mind. I can't seem to do it. Would a hypnotist help? — FRANTIC"

# BIBLIOGRAPHY

Aristotle (*ca.* 350 BCE). *Nicomachean Ethics*, in Loomis L.R. (1943): *Aristotle: On Man in the Universe*, W.J. Black, New York.

Benis, A.M. (1985). *Toward Self & Sanity: On the genetic origins of the human character*, Psychological Dimensions, New York. Revised edition (2008), as *NPA Theory of Personality*, New York, ISBN 978-1312536180.

Benis A.M. (2017). *Geographic Distribution of Genetic Character Traits Based on the NPA Theory of Personality*, KDP/Amazon.

Benis A.M. (2017a). *How Your Personality Type Is Inherited: The NPA Model of Genetic Traits*, KDP/Amazon.

Benis A.M. (2017b). *NPA Personality Theory: The Essentials*, KDP/Amazon.

Benis A.M. (2017c). *NPA Personality Theory in Images*, KDP/Amazon.

Benis A.M. (2018). *The Enigma of Short Parents Who Have Tall Children.* KDP/Amazon.

Benis A.M. (1990). A theory of personality traits leads to a genetic model for borderline types and schizophrenia. *Speculations in Science and Technology* 13 (3), 167-75.

Bosch G. (1970). *Infantile Autism*, Springer-Verlag, New York.

Castelot A. (1965). *Josephine,* Trans. by D. Folliot, Harper and Row, New York.

Herndon W.H. and J.E. Weik (1888). *Life of Lincoln,* Fine Editions Press, Cleveland.

Horney K. (1950). *Neurosis and Human Growth*, Norton, New York.

Horney, K. (1945). *Our Inner Conflicts*, Norton, New York.

James, W. (1890). *Principles of Psychology,* Holt, New York

James, W. (1908). *The Varieties of Religious Experience*, Longmans Green, London.

Le Gallienne E. (1955). *Henrik Ibsen: The Master Builder*, N.Y. University Press, New York.

Maugham W.S. (1951). *The Complete Short Stories*, Heinemann, London.

Maugham W.S. (1939). *Christmas Holiday*, Bantam Books, New York.

Maugham W.S. (1932). *The Narrow Corner,* Doubleday, New York.

Maugham W.S. (1930). *Cakes and Ale,* Doubleday, New York.

Maugham W.S. (1930). *The Gentleman in the Parlour,* Doubleday, New York.

Maugham W.S. (1915). *Of Human Bondage*, Random House, New York.

# SOURCES OF ILLUSTRATIONS

**Plate**

1 Barack Obama by DonkeyHotey. Creative Commons license via Wikipedia Commons File: 2012 Obama Romney caricature.jpg.

2 Vladimir Putin by DonkeyHotey. Creative Commons license via: Wikipedia Commons File: Vladimir Putin - Olympic Host.jpg.

3 Adele Adkins. Digital painting by Carsten S., Berlin, Germany. Creative Commons license via: flickr.com/photos/caschie/ 25600151946.

4 Angela Merkel by DonkeyHotey. Creative Commons license via: flickr.com/photos/donkeyhotey/12952652895.

5 Richard Cheney by DonkeyHotey. Creative Commos license via: flickr.com/photos/donkeyhotey/16011605976.

6 Christopher Christie by DonkeyHotey. Creative Commons license via: flickr.com/photos/donkeyhotey/9529109477.

7 Elizabeth Warren by DonkeyHotey. Creative Commons license via: flickr.com/photos/donkeyhotey/13906218886.

8 Charles Darwin, *ca.* 1854. Filtered image from source photograph in public domain, via Wikipedia Commons File: Charles Darwin seated crop.jpg.

9 Michael Jackson. Wikipedia images via: fr.wikipedia.org/wiki/ Filmographie_de_Michael_Jackson.

10 Resigned type. Adapted from KDP image via: stock.adobe.com.

# INDEX

# ABOUT THE AUTHOR

The author received the degree of Doctor of Science from MIT. His medical training was at the Mount Sinai Medical Center in New York, where he served afterward for many years as Research Associate Professor and Director of Cardiothoracic Intensive Care. He is the author of a number of research papers and review articles. His interest in the genetics of personality grew with his experience with families in the intensive care environment.

www.ingramcontent.com/pod-product-compliance
Lightning Source LLC
Chambersburg PA
CBHW062006280526
45787CB00005B/1997

* 9 7 8 1 5 2 0 9 6 6 9 7 7 *